N'ICE CRE

AVERY
an imprint of Penguin Random House
New York

N'ICE CREAM

80+ RECIPES FOR HEALTHY HOMEMADE VEGAN ICE CREAMS

Virpi Mikkonen and Tuulia Talvio

an imprint of Penguin Random House LLC
375 Hudson Street
New York, New York 10014

Most Avery books are available at special quantity discounts for bulk purchase for sales promotions,
premiums, fund-raising, and educational needs. Special books or book excerpts also can be
created to fit specific needs. For details, write SpecialMarkets@penguinrandomhouse.com.

ISBN 9780735210455

Printed in the United States of America
3rd Printing

Book design by Leena Oravainio

For Axel, Alva, and Finn—the best n'ice
cream test audience in the world

CONTENTS

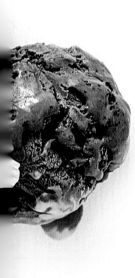

N'ICE CREAM

INTRODUCTION

If you're reading this book, you probably have wild ice cream dreams. You know the ones: where you eat huge, decadent bowls of creamy sundaes and still feel light and happy afterward. Well, guess what? That dream is now turning into reality.

Does that sound too good to be true? Actually, it's just common sense: All you need to do is trade low quality for high quality—and your body will love it! Store-bought ice cream is usually made from highly processed dairy products, refined sugar, and ingredients we don't know how to pronounce, which help ice cream keep for long transit times and during long weeks of sitting in a store freezer. These aren't things you want to put in your body! Luckily, you now have this book, and your ice cream world is about to change.

Who are we to make your ice cream fantasies come true? We are two healthy-food lovers from Finland, a north European country with thousands of lakes and forests—and endless reserves of clean, wild food. We live in Helsinki, a city with a lovely spirit and a quickly growing interest in wholesome eating. Finns are crazy about ice cream and eat lots of it. Despite our cold winters, Finland is actually one of the biggest ice cream consumers in the world!

Sure, we're healthy-food lovers now, but it wasn't always that way. Both of us used to eat store-bought ice cream—and plenty of other store-bought and processed foods. But we felt sick almost every day. Virpi had stomach and skin problems, and Tuulia found out she had celiac disease. Finally, about six years ago, we made the decision to cut out dairy, gluten, and refined sugars from our diets, and shifted to a more wholesome way of eating. We both felt a big difference in our well-being, and we haven't looked back.

We are both ice cream maniacs, and we love to indulge in frozen treats. But after our food awakening, we wanted to make sure what we were eating was wholesome and healthy, not like the stuff we used to eat. So we started creating healthy alternatives and were thrilled to find that they tasted even better than the traditional options we were used to. We soon discovered that fruits and different kinds of plant-based milks and nuts make perfect ice creams. Coconut milk makes a fantastic, smooth base; nuts can provide a dreamy creaminess that'll make you swoon; and natural sweeteners like maple syrup and berries are better than any refined sugar. And a major perk? Each recipe we created required only a few simple ingredients and was quick to throw together! We didn't even need an ice cream maker. As soon as we started eating this way, we couldn't imagine going back.

We had so much fun (and ate so many delicious treats!) making our vegan ice creams that we decided to bring our passions together and create a guide for healthy homemade and plant-based ice creams: a book of all our favorite recipes, such as strawberry cheesecake, chocolate sundae, and mint chocolate ice cream sandwiches. We decided to make the collection an e-book that we could share with our followers, and to our great delight it quickly became very successful. Before we knew it, we were making a real book out of it—which you are now reading.

Why *N'Ice Cream*? All these recipes are free of gluten, refined sugar, and dairy, and most of them are raw, too. The recipes in this book are also vegan, which is a kind way to live—it means caring for your body, the environment, and the animals of the world. When you make these recipes, you're being nice. Plain and simple!

This book was made for all ice cream lovers and people who love to relish without guilt and enjoy wholesome food with rich flavors. Within these pages you'll find more than eighty recipes, all made from pure and natural ingredients. No weird stuff, just good-quality unprocessed or minimally processed ingredients that make you feel good. With these recipes, you will turn a whole new page in your ice cream life and relearn the meaning of real indulgence.

We hope you'll find lots of new ice cream ideas and delicious kitchen adventures within this book. Go ahead and step into the world of n'ice cream! We wish you a pleasant stay, and hope you will make a lot of new ice cream friends!

—Virpi and Tuulia

Without ice cream, there would be darkness and chaos.

–DON KARDONG

THE VEGAN ICE CREAM PANTRY: INGREDIENTS

We think people deserve to eat goodies without feeling crappy afterward. That's why we have selected only wholesome and good-quality ingredients for our recipes. By making ice cream from these ingredients, you can enjoy our treats with a good conscience, a happy belly, and a loving spirit!

Below is a list of the most common ingredients we use. But be ready, too, to find some surprising secret ingredients while flipping through the pages!

It's important to have a good base for your ice cream. Here are some relatively neutral-flavored creamy vegan bases to get you started.

Coconut Milk

Full-fat coconut milk makes a perfect base for homemade ice cream. It's creamy and works well with many different flavors. And don't be afraid of it even if you don't like coconut; when you use other ingredients, such as chocolate or fruit, the coconut flavor is very subtle.

To get a creamy texture, store coconut milk cans in the refrigerator—it separates the solid from the liquid; then just use the thick, solid, white cream. You can save the liquid and use it in smoothies, for example. When you buy coconut milk, choose one with a high amount of coconut, as it will give you more of the thick coconut cream.

Tip! If you're up for an adventure, try making coconut milk at home! You'll find the recipe for Homemade Coconut Milk on page 49.

Plant-Based Milks

Milks made from nuts, rice, or oats are good liquids to use as a base, as they give a nice flavor and creaminess. Try out different kinds of milks and use your favorite one!

Frozen Bananas

Bananas are the ultimate ingredient for easy ice creams—in fact, simply blending plain frozen bananas will give you instant banana ice cream! It's good to favor ripe—and even a little bit overripe—bananas (with black spots), as they give more sweetness and a richer flavor than unripe ones. Besides making "nana n'ice cream," frozen bananas are a good addition to any ice cream mixture, as they bring a bit of sweetness and make the mixture creamier. When freezing bananas, remember to peel and cut them into small pieces before putting in the freezer, as it's hard to chop a frozen banana. We always have some bananas in our freezers so we can use them in so many different treats!

Avocados

Avocado yields a wonderfully rich and creamy texture, and it works especially well with chocolate or by itself with some sweetener and spices.

Nuts and Seeds

When you're craving really creamy and dreamy ice cream, use nuts as one of the main ingredients. Macadamia nuts, soaked cashews, or soaked almonds yield a wonderfully creamy mixture. Or take a shortcut and use a nut butter like peanut or almond. If you're allergic to nuts,

For those with nut allergies: All recipes that don't contain nuts or have a nut-free option are marked with this symbol! (NF) nut free

you can replace nut butters with seed butters for just as much deliciousness. In some recipes, we also use hemp seeds or sesame seeds, which are nutrient rich and flavorful and give a thick texture.

I think we can all agree that ice cream needs to be sweet. Instead of refined sugars, we like to use natural sweeteners, which are gentler on the body. Try these sweeties!

Coconut Palm Syrup

Coconut palm syrup (also called coconut syrup) is made from the nectar of coconut palm blossoms and has a really nice aromatic and caramel taste.

Maple Syrup

Maple syrup is very versatile and has a rich flavor that pairs well with ice creams. When you buy maple syrup, be sure to buy it pure, as you don't want any added sugars or artificial ingredients in it! We like to use grade B maple syrup for its richer flavor—it's delicious in ice creams.

(Other syrups to try include rice syrup and glucose syrup, which have their own unique flavor and work nicely with frozen desserts.)

Natural Stevia

Natural stevia is extracted straight from the stevia plant and is available in liquid and powder forms. Stevia doesn't contain any sugar, but it is very potent, so it makes for a good option when you want to spike up the sweetness because you like your ice cream on the sweeter side but still want to limit your sugar intake.

Fresh Fruits and Berries

The key ingredients to really fresh, flavorful homemade ice creams are fruits and berries. Besides being delicious and naturally sweet, they're totally good for you! Pick any berry you like, combine it with some coconut milk, add a drop of sweetener, and you've got yourself a delicious ice cream mixture. Go for ripe fruits and berries, as they have a lot of flavor and a yummy sweetness. Our favorite

fruit sweetener is fresh dates—
we prefer juicy Medjool dates.

Dried Fruits and Berries

Organic dried dates, figs, apricots,
and raisins dried without sulfur
dioxide are great sweetener options.
Sometimes we like to puree dried
fruits for our ice creams—it adds a
rich texture and a satisfying
sweetness. When we want to add

a hint of caramel and some crunch
to our ice cream, we use dried
mulberries, an ancient and flavorful
superfood.

Hint! As we all prefer a different level
of sweetness, you can (and should!)
taste the ice cream mixture while
making it so you'll achieve the
sweetness level that makes your taste
buds happy.

**Natural, pure spices and herbs bring your ice cream
to life and make it extra delicious! Be brave
and try our favorites, listed here.**

Vanilla

Vanilla is one of the loveliest spices
that you can use in ice cream. We love
to use natural vanilla extract made
from vanilla beans (it's powerful, so
you need only a little bit). We also
use pure vanilla powder (also called
vanilla bean powder), which is the
highly aromatic black powder
made from ground vanilla beans.
Just ¼ teaspoon of vanilla powder
is equal to the seeds of half a vanilla
bean. For the recipes contained
here, you can use vanilla extract,
vanilla powder, or the seeds from
a vanilla bean.

Cacao

We're quite into chocolate, as you'll
see when flipping through the
recipes. For a deep chocolate flavor,
we like to use raw cacao powder,
which is made by cold-pressing
unroasted cacao beans, and has a lot
of nutrients and antioxidants. If you
cannot find raw cacao powder, you
can use dark unsweetened cocoa
powder instead.

In addition to cacao powder, we use
raw cacao nibs in our recipes. They're
roughly ground cacao beans and have
a strong cacao flavor. They can be
used as a topping or mixed into the
ice cream batter to lend the perfect
crunch. But you can use crushed raw

chocolate or very dark chocolate instead of raw cacao nibs, too, if you prefer.

Desiccated, Shredded, and Flaked Coconut

Coconut comes in many forms and textures. We love using coconut meat (dried or not) in our recipes. You can buy dried coconut at the grocery store, or scrape the meat out of a brown coconut if you have one on hand. Desiccated coconut is dried coconut meat; shredded coconut is thin strands of coconut; and flaked coconut is larger coconut pieces. Use whichever you like and is easily available to you—but always go for the unsweetened form.

Matcha Powder

Matcha, a Japanese green tea, has become a popular ingredient in recent years for its flavor and health benefits. Matcha powder is powerful and rich in antioxidants. Try it in our super-yummy recipe on page 73.

Licorice

Licorice flavor is widely known from candies, but it's also an excellent natural spice that is perfect in ice cream. Licorice root has a deliciously rich flavor. You can use a natural powder made from the licorice root or, if you want a stronger taste, try black powder made from licorice root extract. Look for these in your local health store, or order from online health stores.

Fresh Herbs

We love adding fresh herbs to our ice creams: basil, thyme, rosemary— the list goes on! These flavors pair deliciously well with the creamy sweetness of ice cream. Fresh mint is a must for a lovely mint ice cream, though you can also try fresh peppermint for an even perkier flavor.

Spices

We love to add spices to our recipes; they really ramp up the flavor. We always favor natural and organic spices, which are as pure as possible. Some of our favorites include cinnamon, cardamom, and ginger. When you buy cinnamon, always choose Ceylon cinnamon (the "real" cinnamon), which comes from Sri Lanka, has many health benefits, and contains only a trace amount of the unhealthy compound coumarin (compared to the common cassia cinnamon). Chai, gingerbread, and pumpkin pie spice mixes work great, too.

If you want really creamy ice cream, add some good-quality fat! Fat is the most important ingredient when it comes to texture and minimizes the graininess of ice cream. Here are some favorites.

Coconut Butter

Coconut butter (also called coconut manna) is a deliciously thick and creamy sauce made from coconut meat. We sometimes use it instead of nuts to give a creamy texture.

Extra Virgin Coconut Oil

Extra virgin coconut oil is a great ingredient in vegan ice creams. Coconut oil is liquid when warm, which makes it easy to add to the batter, but it solidifies when cool, which helps the ice cream retain a firmer texture.

Raw Cacao Butter

Raw cacao butter is the extracted oil from whole cacao beans and has a mild and soft cocoa flavor. It's especially great in cakes, as it makes their structure quite firm.

Nut Butters, Almond Butter, and Seed Butters

As we explained in the Bases section, nuts and seeds are great ingredients in vegan ice creams. For extra creaminess, add your favorite nut butter or, if you're intolerant of nuts, use a mild seed butter. Nut butters and seed butters are an easy and delicious addition to any frozen treat.

Different kinds of thickeners can be used to improve the texture in vegan ice creams. They are not necessary, but they can make the mixture a bit creamier and smoother by better binding together the ingredients. Here are a few you can try!

Arrowroot

Arrowroot is a starch made from the root of the arrowroot plant. It's a great thickener for all kinds of recipes—particularly ice cream!

Tapioca

Tapioca is a starch made from the tropical cassava (also called manioc) plant root. It's gluten-free and gives a good texture and viscosity to baked goods. Try it out in our Gluten-Free Waffle Ice Cream Cones and Cups (page 197)!

Chia Seeds

Chia seeds form a thick gel when combined with water and can be used as an egg replacement in vegan baking. Chia seeds are one of the crucial ingredients in our homemade waffles.

HOW TO MAKE
ICE CREAM AT HOME

Making ice cream at home is easy, and there are many ways to do it. Here's a breakdown of some different methods, including how to make ice cream without an ice cream maker.

Tools

High-speed blender or food processor: We recommend having a high-speed blender or a food processor in your kitchen, as they're incredibly handy for preparing all kinds of treats. It is also crucial to have one of these machines for making homemade ice cream, since they let you whip all that creamy goodness together quickly and easily.

Freezer-safe container with a lid: Because you'll need somewhere to put the goods! The lid prevents ice crystals from forming.

Ice pop molds and sticks: These are fun if you want to make ice pops.

Ice cream maker: An ice cream maker is a great investment, as it makes creamy ice cream, but it's totally possible to make delicious ice cream even without one. (See tips on pages 16–18.)

This book: Luckily, you've got that one covered.

How to Make Ice Cream Without an Ice Cream Maker

One of our missions is to prove that making ice cream can be super simple, fun, and easy! That is why we offer you loads of recipes for instant ice cream. Instant ice creams are exactly as they sound—ice creams that you can make and then eat immediately. They only require that you have some frozen ingredients on hand and that you have a blender or a food processor. For non-instant ice creams, you can still prepare many delicious versions without an ice cream maker, as all of our creamy ice cream recipes are possible to prepare in the freezer. You just need to remember to stir the ice cream mixture a few times during the freezing process in order to get a creamy, soft result.

Instant Ice Creams

BLENDER METHOD

Use only frozen ingredients and blend everything together in a high-speed blender or a food processor until the mixture is smooth and creamy. You might have to scrape down the sides of the blender or food processor a few times to achieve the perfect texture. You can also add a couple tablespoons of plant-based milk to aid the blending. Serve immediately.

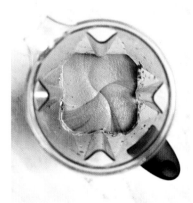

Non-Instant Ice Creams

BLEND-AND-FREEZE METHOD

Prepare the ice cream mixture according to the recipe, pour it into a freezer-safe container with a lid, and freeze. About every 30 minutes for 3 hours, scrape the frozen mixture from the sides of the container and stir vigorously. This will yield that perfect creamy texture. Let thaw for 10 to 15 minutes before serving.

Please note that, with this method, the texture of the ice cream might have more ice crystals than when prepared with an ice cream maker, which blends the mixture continuously and therefore makes it really smooth.

ICE CUBE METHOD

Prepare the ice cream mixture according to the desired recipe. Pour the ice cream mixture into ice cube trays and freeze. When the mixture has frozen, blend the cubes in a high-powered blender or a food processor until smooth and creamy. Add a bit of coconut milk or other plant-based milk, if needed, to make it easier to blend. Serve immediately.

ICE POP METHOD

Prepare the ice cream mixture and pour it into ice pop molds. Place an ice pop stick into each mold so that a little more than half the stick is submerged. Freeze for 4 to 6 hours, or until solid. When the ice cream pops are frozen, run the mold carefully under warm water or dip them into a bowl of warm water to help extract the ice cream pops more smoothly.

Tip! Try using teaspoons as ice cream sticks.

How to Make Ice Cream in an Ice Cream Maker

Though you can make any recipe in this book without one, an ice cream maker is a great investment if you are a serious ice cream lover. Using an ice cream maker gives you nice creamy ice cream quickly and cuts down on ice crystals.

Tips

Remember to freeze the bowl of the ice cream maker according to the manufacturer's instructions.

Before churning the ice cream, make sure the ice cream mixture is cold or at least cool. If it feels warm, refrigerate for a few hours or overnight until cold. You won't be able to make good ice cream from a warm mixture.

Don't fill the bowl of the ice cream maker or the freezer-safe container too much; about two-thirds is good.

When it's ready, the ice cream usually has more of a soft-serve texture. In our opinion, homemade ice creams are best when savored straight after churning. But if you prefer a firmer structure or want to serve it later, freeze the ice cream in a resealable container until solid. Let thaw for 10 to 15 minutes before serving.

How to Store Ice Cream

Store your ice cream in an airtight container in the freezer and use within 1 week (although we think you'll probably devour it in a heartbeat).

Please note: The structure of plant-based homemade ice cream can be a bit different from store-bought ice creams. Plant-based ice creams will become very hard in the freezer because they don't include any additives and because we don't use massive amounts of sugar in them (the sugar keeps the ice cream soft). You'll need to let them thaw for quite a while—15 minutes at least—before serving, if the ice cream has been in the freezer for a long time. Homemade ice creams are always best savored as soon as they are made or within a short time after they've been prepared.

Cool Tips

Toss in some fat. Fat helps you achieve that decadent, rich, and creamy texture. Full-fat coconut milk, nuts, and nut butters are great ingredients to add bulk.

Use a liquid sweetener. When making ice creams, the best sweeteners come in liquid form, like syrups. This helps to prevent icy crystals from forming.

Get the right thickness. You can add richness to the texture of ice cream by using arrowroot powder or another thickener. Nut butters and seed butters work like magic, too!

Keep it cold! Make sure that all your ingredients are cold, or at least cool, before you blend and freeze them, in order to achieve a non-grainy texture.

Cover it up! Cover the bowl or put a lid on your container of ice cream so that ice crystals don't have a chance to form.

Ice cream cravings are not to be taken lightly.

–BETSY CAÑAS GARMON

CREAMY ICE CREAMS

These creamy, dreamy ice creams
will make your heart melt like a scoop
of ice cream on a hot summer day.

Creamy Chocolate-Strawberry
  Ice Pops

Coconut Stracciatella Ice Cream

Creamy Tahini Ice Pops

Avocado 'n' Almond Dream

Blueberry Pie Ice Pops

Almond-Chocolate-Vanilla
  Ice Cream

Avocado–Mint Chocolate Chip
  Ice Cream

Chocolate-Avocado Ice Cream

Chewy Caramel Ice Cream

Raspberry–White Chocolate
  Ice Cream

Creamy Vanilla Ice Cream

Salty Caramel Popcorn Ice Cream

Rose-Cherry Ice Cream

Strawberry Cheesecake
  Ice Cream

Chocolate Creamsicles with
  White Chocolate Glaze

Black Sesame–Licorice Ice Cream

Strawberry-Rhubarb Ice Cream

Raw Chocolate–Covered Cashew
  Ice Cream

Roasted Banana Ice Cream

Mint Chocolate Ice Cream

Pistachio Ice Cream

Strawberry "Froyo"

Matcha–White Chocolate Ice Pops

Date-Cinnamon Ice Cream

Rum and Raisin Ice Cream

CREAMY CHOCOLATE-STRAWBERRY ICE POPS

A collaboration of the classics: strawberry ice cream meets chocolate ice cream. Works every time!

 NF MAKES 4

Chocolate layer:
2 large bananas
2 heaping tablespoons peanut butter or coconut butter
2 tablespoons raw cacao powder or unsweetened cocoa powder
2 tablespoons raw cacao nibs

Strawberry layer:
1 (14-ounce/400-ml) can full-fat coconut milk (refrigerated overnight)
½ teaspoon vanilla powder
2 tablespoons coconut syrup or other sweetener
½ cup strawberries, cut into small pieces

Puree the bananas, peanut butter, and cacao powder in a blender. Add the cacao nibs and mix gently. Pour the mixture into a bowl and set aside.

Open the coconut milk can and scoop the thick white cream into a bowl. Stir in the vanilla powder and coconut syrup. Gently mix in the strawberries.

Pour alternating layers of the chocolate mixture and the strawberry mixture into ice pop molds. Add ice pop sticks and freeze for 4 to 6 hours, until firm. Remove the molds by dipping them into hot water for a moment. Serve and enjoy!

COCONUT STRACCIATELLA ICE CREAM

This dairy-free version of creamy stracciatella is definitely as good as its traditional counterpart, and leaves you feeling refreshed.

SERVES 4

¾ cup (180 ml) cashew nuts (soaked overnight or for at least 4 hours)
1 (14-ounce/400-ml) can full-fat coconut milk
3 to 4 tablespoons maple syrup or other sweetener
1 teaspoon vanilla extract
⅓ cup (70 g/2.5 ounces) raw chocolate or very dark chocolate

Drain and rinse the cashews and put them in a blender with the coconut milk, maple syrup, and vanilla. Blend until creamy and smooth.

Taste, and add more vanilla or sweetener, if desired.

With an ice cream maker: Pour the mixture into an ice cream maker and prepare according to the manufacturer's instructions. While the ice cream is churning, melt the chocolate in a small saucepan set over low heat. Just before the ice cream is ready, pour in the melted chocolate. It will break down into small pieces.

Serve immediately or transfer to a freezer-safe container, cover, and freeze until ready to use. Let the ice cream thaw for 10 to 15 minutes before serving.

Without an ice cream maker: Break the chocolate into small pieces. Pour the ice cream mixture into a freezer-safe bowl, fold in the crushed chocolate, and freeze for about 3 hours, mixing well every 30 minutes. Scoop into bowls, serve, and enjoy!

CREAMY TAHINI ICE POPS

If you like tahini, you're going to love these creamy ice pops. The slightly salty tahini combined with the sweetness of banana and maple syrup is heavenly.

 NF   MAKES   6

2 (14-ounce/400-ml) cans full-fat coconut milk (refrigerated overnight)
1 ripe banana
2 tablespoons tahini
2 tablespoons maple syrup or other sweetener
½ teaspoon vanilla extract

Open the coconut milk cans and scoop out the thick, solid white cream into a blender. Add the banana, tahini, maple syrup, and vanilla and blend until smooth. Taste and add more sweetener or tahini, if desired. Pour the mixture into ice pop molds. Add ice pop sticks and freeze for 4 to 6 hours, until firm. Remove the molds by dipping them into hot water for a moment. Serve and enjoy!

AVOCADO 'N' ALMOND DREAM

We call this one "eating for beauty," as it's loaded with so much goodness from avocados and almonds, two of our favorite beauty foods. You can't help but feel like a total goddess while savoring a scoop!

SERVES 6

2 ripe avocados, peeled and diced
2⅓ cups (580 ml) unsweetened almond milk or other nut milk
3 tablespoons almond butter
6 to 8 fresh dates, pitted
3 tablespoons maple syrup or other sweetener
1 teaspoon vanilla extract

Combine the avocados, almond milk, almond butter, dates, maple syrup, and vanilla in a blender and blend until smooth. The mixture should be thick and very creamy. If the mixture is too thick, add a bit of almond milk, but be careful not to make the mixture too runny. Taste and add more sweetener, if desired.

With an ice cream maker: Pour the mixture into an ice cream maker and prepare according to the manufacturer's instructions. Serve immediately or transfer to a freezer-safe container, cover, and freeze until ready to serve. Let the ice cream thaw for 10 to 15 minutes before serving.

Without an ice cream maker: Pour the ice cream mixture into a freezer-safe bowl and freeze for about 3 hours, mixing well every 30 minutes. Scoop into bowls, serve, and enjoy!

N'Ice Cream

BLUEBERRY
PIE ICE POPS

When you're craving some blueberry pie but are not in the mood to bake, make ice cream!

 NF MAKES 6

1 (14-ounce/400-ml) can full-fat coconut milk (refrigerated overnight)
½ cup (120 ml) fresh blueberries, plus a handful for the ice pop molds
2 to 4 tablespoons maple syrup or other sweetener
½ teaspoon vanilla extract
1 teaspoon ground cardamom

Open the coconut milk can and scoop the thick, solid white cream into a blender. Add the blueberries, maple syrup, vanilla, and cardamom and blend until smooth. Taste and add more sweetener or spices, if desired. Pour a small amount of the blueberry cream into ice pop molds, add a few fresh blueberries to each, and divide the remaining mixture among the ice pop molds. Add ice pop sticks and freeze for 4 to 6 hours, until firm. Remove the molds by dipping them into hot water for a moment. Serve and enjoy!

ALMOND-CHOCOLATE-VANILLA ICE CREAM

The deep chocolate flavor in this decadent dish gets great balance from subtle vanilla swirls.

SERVES **4**

Chocolate ice cream:
2 frozen bananas
3 tablespoons raw cacao powder or unsweetened cocoa powder
2 heaping tablespoons almond butter
1 small handful of almonds
1 tablespoon rice syrup or other sweetener
1 teaspoon vanilla extract
2 tablespoons raw cacao nibs

Vanilla swirl:
1 (14-ounce/400-ml) can full-fat coconut milk (refrigerated overnight)
1 teaspoon vanilla extract
1 tablespoon rice syrup or other sweetener

Combine the bananas, cacao powder, almond butter, almonds, and a little bit of water in a blender. Puree until smooth. Beware of adding too much water—you don't want the mixture to get too runny, as it can make the finished ice cream grainy with small ice crystals. Add the rice syrup, vanilla, and cacao nibs. Stir gently.

To make the vanilla swirl, open the coconut milk cans and scoop the thick white cream into a bowl. Stir in the vanilla and rice syrup. Keep chilled until ready to use.

With an ice cream maker:
Pour the mixture into an ice cream maker and prepare according to the manufacturer's instructions. When the ice cream is almost ready, gently swirl in the vanilla mixture. Serve immediately or transfer to a freezer-safe container, cover, and freeze until ready to serve. Let the ice cream thaw for 10 to 15 minutes before serving.

Without an ice cream maker:
Pour the ice cream mixture into a freezer-safe bowl and freeze for about 3 hours, mixing well every 30 minutes. When the ice cream is almost ready, gently swirl in the vanilla mixture. Scoop into bowls, serve, and enjoy!

AVOCADO-MINT CHOCOLATE CHIP ICE CREAM

Avocado naturally gives a nice flavor to mint ice cream, and a handful of chocolate chips makes this ice cream even more fun to eat.

 NF SERVES 4-6

2 (14-ounce/400-ml) cans full-fat coconut milk (refrigerated overnight)
2 ripe avocados, peeled and diced
5 to 7 tablespoons rice syrup or other sweetener
1 teaspoon peppermint extract
1 large handful of fresh mint leaves
¼ cup (60 ml) raw cacao nibs, unsweetened chocolate chips, or grated raw chocolate

Open the coconut milk cans and scoop the thick white cream into a blender. Add the avocados, rice syrup, peppermint extract, and fresh mint and blend until smooth. Add the cacao nibs and stir with a spoon.

With an ice cream maker:
Pour the mixture into an ice cream maker and prepare according to the manufacturer's instructions. Serve immediately or transfer to a freezer-safe container, cover, and freeze until ready to serve. Let the ice cream thaw for 10 to 15 minutes before serving.

Without an ice cream maker:
Pour the ice cream mixture into a freezer-safe bowl and freeze for about 3 hours, mixing well every 30 minutes. Scoop into bowls, serve, and enjoy!

CHOCOLATE-AVOCADO ICE CREAM

Just add a few spoonfuls of cacao to get a rich creamy chocolate ice cream. Bravo, avocado!

 NF SERVES 4-6

2 (14-ounce/400-ml) cans full-fat coconut milk (refrigerated overnight)
2 ripe avocados, peeled and diced
5 to 7 tablespoons maple syrup or other sweetener
4 to 5 tablespoons raw cacao powder or unsweetened cocoa powder
1 teaspoon vanilla extract

Open the coconut milk cans and scoop the thick white cream into a blender. Add rest of the ingredients and blend until smooth. Taste and add more sweetener or cacao, if desired.

With an ice cream maker:
Pour the mixture into an ice cream maker and prepare according to the manufacturer's instructions. Serve immediately or transfer to a freezer-safe container, cover, and freeze until ready to serve. Let the ice cream thaw for 10 to 15 minutes before serving.

Without an ice cream maker:
Pour the ice cream mixture into a freezer-safe bowl and freeze for about 3 hours, mixing well every 30 minutes. Scoop into bowls, serve, and enjoy!

CHEWY CARAMEL ICE CREAM

If you love chewy toffee, you must try this—caramel ice cream with nut-butter toffee is a match made in ice cream heaven!

SERVES 4

Vanelja's Toffee Candies
(recipe follows)
2 (14-ounce/400-ml) cans
full-fat coconut milk
(refrigerated overnight)
½ cup (120 ml) natural
peanut butter
½ cup (120 ml) fresh dates,
pitted
2 tablespoons extra virgin
coconut oil, melted
½ teaspoon vanilla powder
2 tablespoons arrowroot
powder, or 1 teaspoon
tapioca starch
Coconut syrup, for serving

Prepare the toffee candies first. While the candies are in the refrigerator, prepare the ice cream.

Open the coconut milk cans and scoop the thick white cream into a blender. Add the peanut butter, dates, coconut oil, vanilla, and arrowroot to the blender and blend until smooth.

With an ice cream maker:
Pour the mixture into an ice cream maker and prepare according to the manufacturer's instructions. Serve immediately or transfer to a freezer-safe container, cover, and freeze until ready to serve. Let the ice cream thaw for 10 to 15 minutes before serving. Top with coconut syrup and toffee candies and enjoy!

Without an ice cream maker:
Pour the ice cream mixture into a freezer-safe bowl and freeze for about 3 hours, mixing well every 30 minutes. Scoop into bowls, top with coconut syrup and toffee candies, and enjoy!

These candies are surely addictive!

Vanelja's Toffee Candies

1 cup (240 ml) coconut syrup
1 cup (240 ml) almond butter or other nut butter
Pinch of sea salt

Cover a baking sheet or plate with parchment paper and set aside.

Heat the coconut syrup in a small saucepan over medium heat, stirring continuously, until it starts to foam. Continue to stir for a few minutes. Reduce the heat to low and add the almond butter. Stir the mixture until it begins to thicken slightly and immediately remove from the heat. Pour the warm mixture onto the parchment paper and smooth the surface with a knife or spatula, then sprinkle with the sea salt. Allow the mixture to cool and harden in the refrigerator for 1 hour, then slice the candies into small pieces with a knife.

RASPBERRY-WHITE CHOCOLATE ICE CREAM

The combination of dreamy white chocolate and the fresh taste of raspberries will knock your socks off—trust us.

SERVES 4

¾ cup (180 ml) cashew nuts (soaked overnight or for at least 4 hours)
1 (14-ounce/400 ml) can full-fat coconut milk
½ cup (120 ml) grated raw cacao butter
3 tablespoons maple syrup or other sweetener
1 teaspoon vanilla extract
1 cup (240 ml) fresh or frozen raspberries

Drain and rinse the cashews and put them in a blender with the coconut milk, cacao butter, maple syrup, and vanilla. Blend until creamy and smooth. Taste and add more vanilla or sweetener, if desired.

With an ice cream maker:
Pour the mixture into an ice cream maker and prepare according to the manufacturer's instructions. Just before the ice cream is ready, add the raspberries. Serve immediately or transfer to a freezer-safe container, cover, and freeze until ready to serve. Let the ice cream thaw for 10 to 15 minutes before serving.

Without an ice cream maker:
Pour the ice cream mixture into a freezer-safe bowl, stir in the raspberries, and freeze for about 3 hours, mixing well every 30 minutes. Scoop into bowls, serve, and enjoy!

CREAMY VANILLA ICE CREAM

*Vanilla ice cream is a true classic and loved by many—us included!
It's perfect as it is, or paired with fresh berries or anything
from the Additions and Toppings chapter (page 180).*

SERVES **4**

¾ cup (180 ml) cashew nuts (soaked
overnight)
1 (14-ounce/400-ml) can full-fat coconut
milk, or 1 recipe Homemade Coconut Milk
(recipe follows)
3 to 4 tablespoons maple syrup or other
sweetener
1 teaspoon vanilla extract

Drain and rinse the cashews and put them
in a blender with the coconut milk, maple
syrup, and vanilla. Blend until creamy and
smooth. Taste and add more vanilla or
sweetener, if desired.

With an ice cream maker:
Pour the mixture into an ice cream maker
and prepare according to the manufacturer's
instructions. Serve immediately or transfer
to a freezer-safe container, cover, and freeze
until ready to serve. Let the ice cream thaw
for 10 to 15 minutes before serving.

Without an ice cream maker:
Pour the ice cream mixture into a freezer-
safe bowl and freeze for about 3 hours,
mixing well every 30 minutes. Scoop into
bowls, serve, and enjoy!

Hint! Use vanilla powder instead of vanilla
extract for an authentic vanilla bean-
speckled look. You can even try making
your own coconut milk with our simple
recipe!

Homemade Coconut Milk

  SERVES **4**

2 brown coconuts
3 to 4 cups (about 1 liter) coconut water
or plain water
1 teaspoon vanilla extract, optional

Pierce one "eye" of the coconut with a drill
or sharp knife. Drain the coconut water into
a bowl. Split the coconut by covering it with
a towel and smashing with a hammer.
Remove the coconut meat with a sharp knife
and place the pieces in a high-speed blender.
Add the coconut water and mix until smooth.
Pour the mixture through a nut bag or
muslin/cheesecloth into a jar and squeeze
out as much liquid as possible. Store the
coconut milk in the refrigerator
and use within 1 week.

*Yes, you can
make delicious
coconut milk
at home and
use it in your
ice creams!*

SALTY CARAMEL POPCORN ICE CREAM

Salty meets sweet + crunchy popcorn meets creamy ice cream = highly addictive!

 NF SERVES 4

1 cup (240 ml) popcorn, popped in coconut oil and cooled, plus 1 cup (240 ml) for serving
1 (14-ounce/400-ml) can full-fat coconut milk (refrigerated overnight)
1 cup (240 ml) oat milk or other plant-based milk
5 fresh dates, pitted
2 tablespoons coconut butter
2 tablespoons arrowroot powder
1 teaspoon vanilla extract
Caramel Sauce for serving (page 182)

Combine the popcorn, coconut milk, oat milk, dates, coconut butter, arrowroot, and vanilla in a blender. Blend until smooth and creamy.

With an ice cream maker: Pour the mixture into an ice cream maker and prepare according to the manufacturer's instructions. Serve immediately or transfer to a freezer-safe container, cover, and freeze until ready to serve. Let the ice cream thaw for 10 to 15 minutes before serving.

Without an ice cream maker: Pour the ice cream mixture into a freezer-safe bowl and freeze for about 3 hours, mixing well every 30 minutes.

Scoop the ice cream into bowls, sprinkle with popcorn, and top with the Caramel Sauce. Serve and enjoy!

ROSE-CHERRY ICE CREAM

Cherries and roses are both great aphrodisiacs, so this is the perfect dessert for a great date. It's the most romantic ice cream ever!

SERVES 4

2 frozen bananas
2 cups (480 ml)
unsweetened almond milk
or coconut milk
2 tablespoons coconut
butter or extra virgin
coconut oil
1 teaspoon vanilla extract
1 cup (240 ml) fresh
cherries, pitted
1 teaspoon rose water
1 tablespoon rice syrup or
other sweetener

Combine the bananas, almond milk, coconut butter, and vanilla in a blender and blend until smooth. Pour about one-third of the mixture into a bowl and place in the refrigerator. Add the cherries, rose water, and rice syrup to the remaining two-thirds of the banana mixture and blend until smooth.

With an ice cream maker:
Pour the mixture into an ice cream maker and prepare according to the manufacturer's instructions. When it's almost done, swirl in the reserved banana mixture. Serve immediately or transfer to a freezer-safe container, cover, and freeze until ready to serve. Let the ice cream thaw for 10 to 15 minutes before serving.

Without an ice cream maker:
Pour the ice cream mixture into a freezer-safe bowl and swirl in the reserved banana mixture. Freeze for about 3 hours, mixing well every 30 minutes. Scoop into bowls, serve, and enjoy!

N'Ice Cream

STRAWBERRY CHEESECAKE ICE CREAM

Here's a perfect treat for a sunny day! Strawberry cheesecake is a true summer classic. It's just crying out to be made into ice cream.

SERVES 4

1½ cups (360 ml) fresh strawberries, washed and stems removed
1 banana
1 cup (240 ml) unsweetened almond milk or other plant-based milk
1 teaspoon vanilla extract
1 tablespoon cashew butter or nut butter or seed butter of your choice
1 cup (240 ml) cashew nuts
3 tablespoons arrowroot powder
1 recipe Cake Crumble (page 186)

Chop ¼ cup (60 ml) of the strawberries into small pieces and set aside. Put the remaining strawberries, the banana, almond milk, vanilla, cashew butter, cashews, and arrowroot in a blender and blend until smooth.

Taste and add sweetener or additional vanilla, if desired. Stir in the strawberries.

With an ice cream maker:
Pour the ice cream mixture into an ice cream maker and prepare according to the manufacturer's instructions.

Without an ice cream maker:
Pour the ice cream mixture into a freezer-safe bowl and freeze for about 3 hours, mixing well every 30 minutes.

When the ice cream is ready, scoop out some ice cream balls and roll them in the prepared cake crumble. Serve and enjoy!

CHOCOLATE CREAMSICLES WITH WHITE CHOCOLATE GLAZE

These double-chocolate pops have a dark mysterious soul and a pretty white jacket. Come and meet these creamy charmers and be ready to fall in love!

MAKES 4

2 ripe bananas
3 tablespoons almond butter or nut butter or seed butter of your choice
3 tablespoons raw cacao powder or unsweetened cocoa powder
1 teaspoon vanilla extract
½ cup (120 ml) unsweetened almond milk or other plant-based milk
White Chocolate Sauce (page 182)

Combine all the ingredients except the White Chocolate Sauce in a blender and blend until smooth. Pour the mixture into ice pop molds, add ice pop sticks, and freeze for 4 to 6 hours, until firm.

Line a baking sheet with parchment paper and set aside.

When the creamsicles are solid, remove them from the molds (dip them in hot water for a moment to make this easier) and dip into the White Chocolate Sauce. Transfer to the prepared baking sheet and return them to the freezer for a moment to allow the white chocolate to set. Serve and enjoy!

BLACK SESAME–LICORICE ICE CREAM

Roasted black sesame seeds and licorice give this ice cream its enchanting character. And its black color is simply stunning.

 NF SERVES 4

½ cup (120 ml) black sesame seeds
2 (14-ounce/400-ml) cans full-fat coconut milk (refrigerated overnight)
1 cup (240 ml) unsweetened almond milk or other plant-based milk
3 to 5 tablespoons licorice root powder or grated licorice root stick
⅓ cup (80 ml) coconut palm syrup or other sweetener
3 tablespoons arrowroot powder
1 teaspoon vanilla extract

Toast the sesame seeds lightly on a dry pan, pour into a blender, and let cool for a couple of minutes.

Open the coconut milk cans and scoop the thick white cream into the blender. Add the remaining ingredients and blend until smooth.

With an ice cream maker:
Pour the mixture into an ice cream maker and prepare according to the manufacturer's instructions. Serve immediately or transfer to a freezer-safe container, cover, and freeze until ready to serve. Let the ice cream thaw for 10 to 15 minutes before serving.

Without an ice cream maker:
Pour the ice cream mixture into a freezer-safe bowl and freeze for about 3 hours, mixing well every 30 minutes. Scoop into bowls, serve, and enjoy!

Hint! Find licorice root powder in your local health food store or order it online.

STRAWBERRY-RHUBARB ICE CREAM

Rhubarb is the ultimate sign of summer and tastes great as is. But paired with strawberries and coconut and made into a creamy ice cream . . . you're going to be in summer heaven!

 NF SERVES 4

2 big stalks rhubarb
1 (14-ounce/400-ml) can full-fat coconut milk (refrigerated overnight)
1 tablespoon cashew butter or coconut butter
1 tablespoon extra virgin coconut oil
3 tablespoons coconut palm syrup or other sweetener
½ teaspoon vanilla extract
1 cup (240 ml) chopped fresh strawberries

Chop the rhubarb into small pieces. Open the coconut milk can and scoop the thick white cream into a blender. Add the rhubarb, cashew butter, coconut oil, coconut syrup, vanilla, and ½ cup (120 ml) of the strawberries. Blend until smooth and creamy. Taste and add more sweetener, if desired.

With an ice cream maker:
Pour the mixture into an ice cream maker and prepare according to the manufacturer's instructions. Just before the ice cream is ready, add the remaining ½ cup (120 ml) strawberries. Serve immediately or transfer to a freezer-safe container, cover, and freeze until ready to serve. Let the ice cream thaw for 10 to 15 minutes before serving.

Without an ice cream maker:
Pour the ice cream mixture into a freezer-safe bowl and freeze for about 3 hours, mixing well every 30 minutes. Just before the ice cream is ready, add the remaining ½ cup (120 ml) strawberries. Scoop the ice cream into bowls, serve, and enjoy!

RAW CHOCOLATE-COVERED CASHEW ICE CREAM

Who could resist a classic Magnum-style ice cream? And why would you want to, when you can make it so easily and with such great ingredients?

MAKES 4

1 (14-ounce/400-ml) can full-fat coconut milk (refrigerated overnight)
2 tablespoons cashew butter
2 tablespoons maple syrup or other sweetener
½ teaspoon vanilla extract

Chocolate glaze:
½ cup raw cacao butter
2 tablespoons extra virgin coconut oil
3 tablespoons maple syrup or other sweetener
5 tablespoons raw cacao powder

Open the coconut milk can and scoop the thick white cream into a blender. Add the cashew butter, maple syrup, and vanilla and blend until smooth. Taste and add more sweetener, if desired. Pour into ice pop molds, add ice pop sticks, and freeze for 4 to 6 hours, until solid.

Line a baking sheet with parchment paper and set aside.

To make the chocolate glaze, melt the cacao butter and coconut oil in a small saucepan over medium-low heat. Remove from the heat, add the maple syrup and cacao powder, and whisk into a smooth sauce. Taste and add more sweetener or cacao, if desired. Pour into a bowl or cup.

Take the ice pops from the freezer. Remove the molds and dip the ice pops quickly into the chocolate glaze. Set them on the prepared baking sheet and return to the freezer until the glaze is set. Serve and enjoy!

ROASTED BANANA ICE CREAM

If you've never had roasted bananas, you're in for a treat. The natural sweetness of bananas is brought out in force when you roast them. If you love that sweet, creamy flavor, then it's a good bet that this ice cream will be your new best friend.

NF SERVES 6

5 very ripe bananas
2 teaspoons ground Ceylon cinnamon
½ cup (120 ml) full-fat coconut milk
1½ cups (360 ml) unsweetened almond milk or other nut milk
1 teaspoon vanilla extract
½ cup (120 ml) raw cacao nibs or crushed raw chocolate
Maple syrup, for serving

Preheat the oven to 350°F (175°C). Line a baking sheet with parchment paper and set aside.

Slice the bananas into 1-inch (2 to 3-cm) pieces and spread them on the prepared baking sheet.

Sprinkle the bananas with the cinnamon. Bake for 30 minutes, turning once halfway through, until the bananas are brown and soft. Remove from the oven and let cool completely, 30 to 45 minutes.

Combine the bananas, coconut milk, almond milk, and vanilla in a blender and blend until smooth. Taste and add more cinnamon or a splash of sweetener, if desired. Add the cacao nibs and stir with a spoon.

With an ice cream maker:
Pour the mixture into an ice cream maker and prepare according to the manufacturer's instructions. Serve immediately or transfer to a freezer-safe container, cover, and freeze until ready to serve. Let the ice cream thaw for 10 to 15 minutes. Scoop ice cream into bowls, drizzle with maple syrup, and serve.

Without an ice cream maker:
Pour the ice cream mixture into a freezer-safe bowl and freeze for about 3 hours, mixing well every 30 minutes. Scoop into bowls, drizzle with maple syrup, and enjoy!

MINT CHOCOLATE ICE CREAM

*Creamy chocolate ice cream with a hint of peppermint:
It's simple and always stylish.*

SERVES 4

1½ cups (360 ml) macadamia nuts
2 cups (480 ml) unsweetened almond milk or full-fat coconut milk
2 tablespoons extra virgin coconut oil, melted
5 fresh dates, pitted
5 tablespoons raw cacao powder or unsweetened cocoa powder
1 teaspoon vanilla extract
Few drops of peppermint extract, or about 5 large fresh peppermint leaves

Combine all the ingredients in a blender and blend until smooth.

With an ice cream maker:
Pour the mixture into an ice cream maker and prepare according to the manufacturer's instructions. Serve immediately or transfer to a freezer-safe container, cover, and freeze until ready to serve. Let the ice cream thaw for 10 to 15 minutes before serving.

Without an ice cream maker:
Pour the ice cream mixture into a freezer-safe bowl and freeze for about 3 hours, mixing well every 30 minutes. Scoop into bowls, serve, and enjoy!

PISTACHIO ICE CREAM

*Looking for something festive and totally delicious? This rich
and creamy pistachio ice cream is definitely the answer.
One bite, and you'll be craving more!*

SERVES 6

1½ cups (360 ml) shelled pistachios
1½ cups (360 ml) full-fat coconut milk
1½ cups (360 ml) unsweetened almond milk or other nut milk
6 fresh dates, pitted
½ teaspoon vanilla extract
3 to 4 tablespoons maple syrup or other sweetener

Put the pistachios in a blender (or use a food processor for this step) and grind into a flour. Add all the remaining ingredients and blend until smooth. Taste and add more sweetener, if needed.

With an ice cream maker:
Pour the mixture into an ice cream maker and prepare according to the manufacturer's instructions. Serve immediately or transfer to a freezer-safe container, cover, and freeze until ready to serve. Let the ice cream thaw for 10 to 15 minutes before serving.

Without an ice cream maker:
Pour the ice cream mixture into a freezer-safe bowl and freeze for about 3 hours, mixing well every 30 minutes. Scoop into bowls, serve, and enjoy!

STRAWBERRY "FROYO"

This simple "froyo" is all about strawberries.
The more strawberries, the better!

 NF SERVES 4

1 (14-ounce/400-ml) can
full-fat coconut milk
(refrigerated overnight)
2 cups (480 ml) fresh
strawberries, stems
removed and cut
into pieces
3 to 4 tablespoons maple
syrup or other sweetener

Open the coconut milk can
and scoop the thick white
cream into a blender. Add
the strawberries and
maple syrup and blend
until smooth. Taste and
add more sweetener, if
desired.

With an ice cream maker:
Pour the mixture into an
ice cream maker and
prepare according to
the manufacturer's
instructions. Serve
immediately or transfer to
a freezer-safe container,
cover, and freeze until
ready to serve. Let the ice
cream thaw for 10 to 15
minutes before serving.

*Without an ice cream
maker:*
Pour the ice cream mixture
into a freezer-safe bowl
and freeze for about
3 hours, mixing well every
30 minutes. Scoop into
bowls, serve, and enjoy!

MATCHA–WHITE CHOCOLATE ICE POPS

For all you matcha lovers, these creamy pops are all about that wonderful (and powerful!) green tea. And to make these pops a bit more fabulous, glaze them with a delicious raw white chocolate sauce.

SERVES 4-6

½ cup (120 ml) macadamia nuts
1 (14-ounce/400-ml) can full-fat coconut milk
1 teaspoon matcha powder
1 to 2 tablespoons maple syrup or other sweetener
½ teaspoon vanilla extract
White Chocolate Sauce (page 182), for glazing

Combine all the ingredients except the White Chocolate Sauce in a blender and blend until smooth. Taste and add more sweetener or matcha, if desired. Pour into ice pop molds, add ice pop sticks, and freeze for 4 to 6 hours, until solid.

Line a baking sheet with parchment and set aside.

When the ice pops are frozen, remove them from the freezer. Loosen the molds by quickly dipping each mold in hot water. Working quickly, dip each ice pop in the White Chocolate Sauce to coat. Place the ice pops on the prepared baking sheet and place the sheet in the freezer to set the glaze. Serve and enjoy!

DATE-CINNAMON ICE CREAM

The warm notes of cinnamon in this date-sweetened ice cream are gentle and comforting.

 NF SERVES 2

Date swirl:
8 fresh dates, pitted
2 tablespoons extra virgin coconut oil
5 tablespoons water
½ teaspoon vanilla extract
Pinch sea salt

Coconut Cream:
1½ cups (360 ml) coconut flakes or shredded coconut or the flesh from a mature coconut
3 tablespoons extra virgin coconut oil

Ice cream:
1 (14-ounce/400-ml) can full-fat coconut milk
2 teaspoons ground Ceylon cinnamon
3 fresh dates, pitted
½ teaspoon vanilla powder

To make the date swirl, combine all the ingredients in a blender and blend until smooth. Add more water if needed to achieve the consistency of a smooth caramel sauce. Set aside.

To make the coconut cream using a blender or food processor, pulse the coconut flakes to a powder. Continue pulsing until the mixture starts to hold together. Add the coconut oil and blend to the consistency of a smooth butter. (If you don't have a high-speed blender, you can also use store-bought coconut manna.)

(recipe continues)

To make the ice cream, put 1 cup (240ml) of the Coconut Cream, the coconut milk, cinnamon, dates, and vanilla into the blender and blend until smooth. Spoon the date swirl into the ice cream and mix gently.

With an ice cream maker:
Pour the ice cream mixture into an ice cream maker and prepare according to the manufacturer's instructions. Serve immediately or transfer to a freezer-safe container, cover, and freeze until ready to serve. Scoop into bowls, serve, and enjoy!

Without an ice cream maker:
Pour the ice cream mixture into a freezer-safe bowl and freeze for about 3 hours, mixing well every 30 minutes. Scoop into bowls, serve, and enjoy!

Quick tip! Instead of homemade coconut cream, you can also use 1 (14-ounce/400-ml) can full-fat coconut milk, refrigerated overnight—just use the white, thick stuff from the can. You can also skip the date swirl by adding all the dates straight into the ice cream batter, if you want to simplify this recipe!

RUM AND RAISIN ICE CREAM

*Rich chocolate ice cream flavored with raisins
marined in rum is a perfect adult treat.*

 NF SERVES 4

2 tablespoons almond
liqueur or other liqueur
5 tablespoons rum
3 tablespoons organic
raisins
3 bananas, peeled, cut
into small coins, and
frozen overnight or for at
least 4 hours
1½ tablespoons raw cacao
powder or unsweetened
cocoa powder
1 teaspoon vanilla extract
1 tablespoon coconut
syrup or other sweetener
3 tablespoons raw
cacao nibs

Pour the almond liqueur
and rum into a small pot
and bring to a boil.
Remove from the heat,
add the raisins, and let
soak for at least 4 hours
or overnight.

Place the bananas in a
blender and pulse until
crumbled. Continue
pulsing until the bananas
start to form a smooth
texture, scraping down
the sides of the blender if
necessary. Add the raisins,
cacao powder, vanilla, and
coconut syrup and pulse
until smooth and creamy.
Mix in the raw cacao nibs
and stir with a spoon.
Scoop into bowls, serve,
and enjoy!

Tip! If the ice cream melts too
much while you process it, you
can freeze it to harden a bit
before serving.

INSTANT ICE CREAMS

If you need a quick fix, try these fast ice creams!

Banana Ice Creams

Mocha Sundae

Raspberry-Licorice Ice Cream

Dreamy Chocolate Sundae

Cinnamon Bun Ice Cream

Raspberry Delight

Mango–Passion Fruit Tropical Delight

Blueberry Ice Cream with White Chocolate–Cardamom Sauce

Coconut Sundae

Sweet Potato–Gingerbread Ice Cream

Fresh Berry Sorbet

Choco-Vanilla Bomb

Mint Chocolate Chip Sundae

Black Currant–Vanilla Ice Cream

Spa Slush

Mango-Melon Sorbet

Caramel-Lingonberry Soft Serve in Oat Bowls

BANANA ICE CREAMS

For a quick and easy ice cream, just throw some frozen bananas into a blender, whip them up, and enjoy. Don't be afraid of the black spots on overripe bananas—just peel 'em, chop 'em, toss 'em in the freezer, and wait for an ice cream craving to strike!

 NF · SERVES 1

Basic Banana Ice Cream

2 frozen bananas
2 to 3 tablespoons unsweetened almond milk or other plant-based milk, if needed
¼ teaspoon vanilla extract

Strawberry-Banana Ice Cream

1 frozen banana
1 cup (240 ml) frozen strawberries
2 to 3 tablespoons unsweetened almond milk or other plant-based milk, if needed

Chocolate-Banana Ice Cream

2 frozen bananas
2 to 3 tablespoons unsweetened almond milk or other plant-based milk, if needed
1½ tablespoons raw cacao powder or unsweetened cocoa powder
1 tablespoon coconut palm syrup or other sweetener

Peel the bananas and cut them into small coins. Put the bananas in an airtight container and freeze for at least 4 hours, or overnight.

Combine the bananas (and other fruit) in a blender and pulse until smooth, scraping down the sides of the blender as necessary. If the mixture is too thick, add the almond milk to achieve the desired consistency. Add flavoring and sweetener, if using, and blend until combined. Scoop into a bowl, serve, and enjoy!

MOCHA SUNDAE

Even if you're not a coffee drinker, you really should try this heavenly coffee sundae. The creamy, rich taste is out of this world.

SERVES 2

1 cup (240 ml) cashew nuts
½ cup (120 ml) unsweetened almond milk or other plant-based milk
3 frozen bananas
3 tablespoons almond butter
1 tablespoon instant coffee, plus more for serving
Coconut Whipped Cream (page 185), for serving, optional
Raw cacao nibs, for serving

Place the cashews in a blender and pulse to a fine powder. Add the almond milk and blend until smooth. Add the frozen bananas, almond butter, and instant coffee and blend until smooth. Scoop into serving bowls, top with Coconut Whipped Cream (if using), sprinkle with some instant coffee and cacao nibs, serve, and enjoy!

RASPBERRY-LICORICE ICE CREAM

The subtle taste of licorice makes this ice cream totally unique—and totally addictive!

 NF SERVES 2

1 (14-ounce/400-ml) can full-fat coconut milk (refrigerated overnight)
½ cup (120 ml) frozen raspberries
1 frozen banana
3 fresh dates, pitted
½ teaspoon vanilla extract
1 to 2 teaspoons licorice root powder
Licorice Cream (recipe follows), for serving
Handful of raspberries, for serving

Open the coconut milk can and scoop the thick white cream into a blender. Add the raspberries, banana, dates, vanilla, and licorice powder and blend until smooth, scraping down the sides of the blender as necessary. Taste and add more licorice powder, if desired. Scoop into a bowl, top with Licorice Cream and raspberries, and enjoy!

Licorice Cream

6 fresh dates, pitted
2 tablespoons maple syrup
¾ cup (180 ml) unsweetened almond milk or other plant-based milk
2 to 3 teaspoons licorice root powder

Chop the dates into smaller pieces. Combine all the ingredients in a blender and blend until smooth. Taste and add more licorice powder, if desired.

DREAMY CHOCOLATE SUNDAE

We all get a strong chocolate craving sometimes. It's good to have this recipe in your back pocket for handling those emergencies!

 SERVES 2

1 (14-ounce/400-ml) can full-fat coconut milk (refrigerated overnight)
2 frozen bananas
2 to 3 tablespoons raw cacao powder or unsweetened cocoa powder
1 tablespoon almond butter or other nut or seed butter
1 to 2 tablespoons maple syrup or other sweetener
½ teaspoon vanilla extract
Coconut Whipped Cream (page 185), for serving
Chocolate Sauce (page 182), for serving
Fresh cherries, for serving

Open the coconut milk can and scoop the thick white cream into a blender. Add the bananas, cacao powder, almond butter, maple syrup, and vanilla and blend until smooth, scraping down the sides of the blender, as necessary. Taste and add more sweetener or cacao powder, if desired. Scoop into bowls, decorate with Coconut Whipped Cream, Chocolate Sauce, and cherries, and enjoy!

CINNAMON BUN ICE CREAM

Cinnamon buns are like a big warm hug from the inside. There is no better comfort food than this ice cream when you are in need of some extra care and tenderness.

SERVES 2

¼ cup (60 ml) almonds
¼ cup (60 ml) pecans
1 teaspoon ground Ceylon cinnamon
½ teaspoon ground cardamom
5 fresh dates, pitted
¼ cup (60 ml) water
3 frozen bananas
3 tablespoons coconut milk
1 teaspoon vanilla extract

Combine the almonds, pecans, cinnamon, and cardamom in a blender and blend until they form a fine crust. Add 1 date and blend until the mixture is still dry but just beginning to form clumps. Scoop half the mixture into a bowl and set aside. Add the remaining dates and the water to the blender and blend to a smooth paste. Scoop the cinnamon paste into a second bowl and set aside.

Wash and dry the blender. Combine the frozen bananas, coconut milk, and vanilla in the blender and blend until smooth. Scoop the ice cream into a bowl. Stir in some of the cinnamon paste. Divide the ice cream between serving bowls and top with chunks of the flaky cinnamon crumbs. Serve and enjoy!

RASPBERRY DELIGHT

This pink berry delight is super easy, fresh, and so creamy. The recipe works perfectly with other berries and fruits as well!

SERVES

1 frozen banana
¾ cup (180 ml) frozen raspberries
1 tablespoon almond butter or other nut or seed butter
1 tablespoon maple syrup or other sweetener
2 to 3 tablespoons unsweetened almond milk or other plant-based milk, optional

Combine the banana, raspberries, almond butter, and syrup in a blender and blend to a smooth and creamy texture, scraping down the sides of the blender a few times if necessary. Add the almond milk, if needed, to achieve the desired texture. Scoop into a bowl, serve, and enjoy!

MANGO–PASSION FRUIT TROPICAL DELIGHT

When the weather turns cold and the days feel shorter, and you find yourself thinking wistfully of those sun-soaked easy days at the beach—make this Tropical Delight and treat yourself to a delicious mini holiday.

SERVES 2

1 (14-ounce/400-ml) can full-fat coconut milk (refrigerated overnight)
1 frozen banana
1 cup (240 ml) frozen mango
½ teaspoon vanilla extract
1 to 2 tablespoons coconut syrup or other sweetener
3 passion fruits
Chocolate Cookie Cups (page 194), for serving, optional

Open the coconut milk can and scoop out the thick white cream into a blender. Add the banana, mango, vanilla, and coconut syrup and blend until smooth, scraping down the sides of the blender as necessary. Taste and add more sweetener, if desired. Reserving 1 passion fruit for decorating, scoop the pulp of 2 passion fruits into the blender and stir the mixture with a spoon. Serve in Chocolate Cookie Cups or regular bowls, top with the pulp from the reserved passion fruit, and enjoy!

BLUEBERRY ICE CREAM WITH WHITE CHOCOLATE–CARDAMOM SAUCE

This one is simple and satisfying—and loaded with flavor! We like to make this ice cream with wild bilberries, which are packed with vitamins, but you can always use regular blueberries. And if you'd like to add some Nordic goodness, just add a bit of wild bilberry powder!

 NF SERVES 2

½ cup (120 ml)
full-fat coconut milk
(refrigerated overnight)
2 frozen bananas
⅔ cup (160 ml) wild
bilberries, or ⅔ cup
(160 ml) blueberries plus 1
tablespoon bilberry powder
½ teaspoon vanilla extract
Splash of coconut syrup
or other sweetener,
if needed
White Chocolate
Cardamom Sauce

Open the coconut milk
can and scoop ½ cup of
the thick white cream and
add it into a blender. Add
the bananas, bilberries,
and vanilla and blend until
smooth. Taste and add
sweetener, if desired.
Serve immediately as

a soft serve or pour into a
freezer-safe bowl with a
lid and freeze for about
1 hour. Scoop into bowls,
drizzle with the White
Chocolate Cardamom
Sauce, and enjoy!

White Chocolate–Cardamom Sauce

½ cup (120 ml) grated raw
cacao butter
¼ cup (60 ml) coconut
butter or cashew butter,
or ½ cup (120 ml) soaked
cashew nuts
¼ cup (60 ml) full-fat
coconut milk
1 to 3 tablespoons coconut
syrup or other sweetener
½ teaspoon vanilla
extract

½ teaspoon ground
cardamom

Melt the cacao butter
in a small saucepan over
medium-low heat. Transfer
to a blender, add the
remaining ingredients, and
blend until smooth. Taste
and add more sweetener
or spices, if desired.

Bilberry facts! Bilberries are a
relative of blueberries. They're
native to north Europe, where
they grow in forests, mainly in
Nordic countries. They are more
nutrient rich than blueberries,
and their taste is a bit more
intense. You can find frozen
bilberries in ethnic European
food stores or you can replace
them with blueberries.

N'Ice Cream

COCONUT SUNDAE

*Ice cream sundaes have a lovely nostalgic vibe, and this quick
version of a vanilla sundae is unbelievably easy,
yet so creamy. You need only four or five ingredients!*

SERVES 2

1 (14-ounce/400-ml) can
full-fat coconut milk
(refrigerated overnight)
2 frozen bananas
½ teaspoon vanilla
extract
1 tablespoon maple syrup,
optional
Peanut Butter–Caramel
Sauce (recipe follows), for
serving

Open the coconut milk
can and scoop the thick,
solid white cream into a
blender. Add the bananas
and vanilla and blend until
smooth, scraping down
the sides of the blender as
necessary. Taste and add
maple syrup, if desired.

Pour into bowls, top with
Peanut Butter–Caramel
Sauce, and enjoy!

Peanut Butter–Caramel Sauce

1 tablespoon peanut
butter
1 tablespoon maple syrup
or other sweetener
2 tablespoons unsweetened
almond milk or other
plant-based milk

Combine all the ingredients
in a small bowl and stir
until you get a nice thick
caramel sauce.

SWEET POTATO-GINGERBREAD ICE CREAM

*It may sound odd, but sweet potato serves as a terrific base for ice cream.
We love to combine it with the warm notes of gingerbread spice
for an autumnal flair—but sweet potato would also work
as a base for rich chocolate ice creams.*

SERVES **2**

1 sweet potato, steamed, mashed,
and frozen in ice cube trays, or
1 cup frozen sweet potato puree
1 frozen banana
4 fresh dates, pitted
2 tablespoons almond butter or
other nut or seed butter
½ cup (120 ml) full-fat coconut milk
1½ teaspoons ground Ceylon
cinnamon
1 teaspoon ground ginger
1 teaspoon ground cardamom

Combine all the ingredients in a
blender and blend until smooth.
Enjoy as a soft serve or transfer to
a bowl and freeze for 1 to 2 hours
before serving.

N'Ice Cream

FRESH BERRY SORBET

This dish does double duty as dessert and a pure vitamin boost!

 NF SERVES 2

1 orange, peeled, pith removed,
and seeded
½ cup (120 ml) frozen red currants
1 cup (240 ml) frozen strawberries
¼ cup red currants, for serving

Combine all the ingredients in a
blender and blend until you get a
smooth and creamy ice cream
texture, scraping down the sides of
the blender a few times if necessary.
Scoop into bowls, serve with red
currants, and enjoy!

CHOCO-VANILLA BOMB

It's a true miracle that something as heavenly as this is made only from natural ingredients. This one's a bomb of total deliciousness!

SERVES 2

4 frozen bananas
⅓ cup (80 ml) unsweetened almond milk or other plant-based milk
2 fresh dates, pitted
1 teaspoon vanilla extract
2 to 3 tablespoons raw cacao powder or unsweetened cocoa powder
2 tablespoons peanut butter or other nut butter or seed butter, plus extra for serving
Pinch of sea salt
Splash of unsweetened almond milk, optional
Fresh berries, for serving

Combine the bananas, almond milk, dates, and vanilla in a blender and blend until smooth, scraping down the sides of the blender as necessary. Transfer half the vanilla mixture to a bowl and set aside.

Add the raw cacao powder, peanut butter, and salt to the remaining vanilla mixture and blend until smooth, adding a splash of almond milk, if needed, to create a smooth texture. Pour the vanilla and chocolate mixtures alternately into bowls, serve with some extra peanut butter and fresh berries, and enjoy!

MINT CHOCOLATE CHIP SUNDAE

Need a mint fix but don't want to wait?
This beauty is ready in minutes!

 NF SERVES 2

1 (14-ounce/400-ml) can full-fat coconut milk (refrigerated overnight)
2 frozen bananas
¼ teaspoon spirulina, optional (for color)
1 tablespoon maple syrup or other sweetener
Handful of fresh mint leaves
Small drop of peppermint extract
⅓ cup (80 ml) raw cacao nibs or grated raw/dark chocolate

Open the coconut milk can and scoop the thick white cream into a blender. Add the bananas, spirulina, if using, maple syrup, fresh mint, and peppermint extract and blend until smooth, scraping down the sides of the blender if necessary. Taste and add more sweetener or mint, if desired. Add about two-thirds of the raw cacao nibs and stir gently with a spoon. Scoop into bowls, sprinkle the remaining raw cacao nibs on top, and enjoy!

BLACK CURRANT-VANILLA ICE CREAM

Mix black currants with coconut milk and banana, and you've got one heck of a dessert. The cardamom and vanilla take it to another level.

SERVES 2

1 cup (240 ml) frozen black currants
1 frozen banana
½ cup (120 ml) full-fat coconut milk
3 fresh dates, pitted
1 teaspoon vanilla powder, or seeds
from 1 vanilla bean
½ teaspoon ground cardamom

Combine all the ingredients in a blender and blend until smooth. Serve and enjoy!

SPA SLUSH

This super-fresh and sweetener-free sorbet is a perfect option when you are looking for a cooling treat with health benefits. It is detox dessert number one!

SERVES 2

3 cucumbers, peeled, seeded, and frozen
1 green apple, cored, sliced, and frozen
Juice of 1 lime
3 fresh basil leaves
A splash of coconut syrup or other sweetener, optional

Combine the cucumbers, apple slices, lime juice, and basil in a blender. Blend until the mixture is a smooth slush. Add sweetener, if desired. Serve and enjoy!

Note! You can also make the slush from non-frozen cucumber and apples by blending all the ingredients in a blender and then running the mixture in an ice cream maker for about 15 minutes.

MANGO-MELON SORBET

It never ceases to amaze us how you can make such a creamy sorbet with only fresh fruits. Mango and melon blend together beautifully in this recipe—like a charm!

 NF SERVES 2

½ frozen peeled honeydew melon or cantaloupe
1 cup (240 ml) frozen mango
1 to 2 frozen bananas
1 tablespoon coconut syrup or other sweetener

Combine all the ingredients in a food processor or high-speed blender and blend until smooth. You can also puree the ingredients in smaller batches, which can make the blending easier. Serve and enjoy!

CARAMEL-LINGONBERRY SOFT SERVE IN OAT BOWLS

Lingonberries and oats are traditional ingredients in our native Finland. This ice cream is a love letter to our home country. When you mix these two classic Finnish flavors with a few more exotic ingredients, you get a simple and tasty treat with pure and perky highlights.

 NF SERVES 4

1½ cups (360 ml) frozen lingonberries, plus more for serving
2 frozen bananas
2 tablespoons rice syrup or other sweetener
½ cup (120 ml) full-fat coconut milk (refrigerated overnight)
½ teaspoon vanilla powder
Oat Ice Cream Bowls (page 190), for serving
Caramel Sauce (page 182), for serving

Combine the lingonberries, bananas, rice syrup, coconut milk, and vanilla powder in a blender and blend until smooth. Taste and add more sweetener, if desired. Scoop the ice cream into the oat bowls, top with Caramel Sauce, and decorate with a few lingonberries. Serve and enjoy!

Lingonberry facts!
Lingonberries, a distant cousin of cranberries, are a very common treat from Scandinavian forests. Their taste is tart and sour, but slightly sweet. You can find frozen lingonberries at ethnic European food stores. You can also replace lingonberries in this recipe with cranberries.

3

ICE POPS AND SORBETS

Cool down, hottie, and take an ice pop or spoon some sorbet!

COCONUT WATER COOLERS

When you need to cool down, make this simple and super-refreshing combo with coconut water, fruits, and berries!

 NF MAKES 6

1 to 2 kiwifruit, peeled and chopped into small pieces
½ cup (120 ml) fresh strawberries, cut into small pieces
½ cup (120 ml) fresh blueberries
1½ cups (360 ml) coconut water

Combine the kiwi and the berries in a bowl. Divide the berry mixture among six ice pop molds and fill the molds with coconut water. Add ice pop sticks and freeze for 4 to 6 hours, until firm. Remove the molds by dipping them into hot water for a moment. Serve and enjoy!

APPLE-AVOCADO-MINT POPS

*Like a green smoothie, but in the form of ice cream—
how great is that? These ice pops are like little
pieces of magic on a very hot day.*

 NF MAKES 4

1 cup (240 ml) freshly pressed apple
juice (from about 3 apples)
1 banana
½ ripe avocado, peeled and diced
5 large fresh mint leaves

Combine all the ingredients in a
blender and blend until smooth
and creamy. Taste and add more
mint, if desired. Pour into ice pop
molds, add ice pop sticks, and
freeze for 4 to 6 hours, until firm.
Remove the molds by dipping them
into hot water for a moment. Serve
and enjoy!

CHOCO BANANAS

*These crazy-good choco-banana ice pops are simple and stylish,
perfect for parties and loved by both kids and adults.*

 NF MAKES 6

3 ripe but firm bananas
½ cup (120 ml) toppings
of your choice: dried
pomegranate seeds,
chopped pistachios and
almonds, desiccated
coconut, raw cacao
nibs, etc.

Chocolate glaze:
½ cup (120 ml) raw cacao
butter
2 tablespoons extra
virgin coconut oil
3 tablespoons maple
syrup or other sweetener
5 tablespoons raw cacao
powder or unsweetened
cocoa powder

Cut the bananas in half
crosswise. Put ice pop

sticks down their centers
and place them in the
freezer on some
parchment paper (to avoid
sticking). While they
harden, choose your
favorite toppings and
assemble them on plates.

To make the chocolate
glaze, melt the cacao
butter and coconut oil
in a small saucepan over
medium-low heat. Remove
from the heat, add the
maple syrup and cacao
powder, and whisk into a
smooth sauce. Taste and
add more sweetener or
cacao, if desired. Pour
into a bowl or cup.

Take the bananas from
the freezer. One by one,
dip the bananas into the
chocolate glaze and roll
them quickly in the chosen
toppings. Set the bananas
back on the parchment
paper and return to the
freezer for a moment to
set the glaze (if you like
a thicker glaze, dip them
again after the first layer
sets). Serve and enjoy!

Hint! You can also use your
favorite raw chocolate or a
good-quality dark chocolate
for the glazing—just melt it
and you're ready
to dip and decorate!

STRAWBERRY-BASIL CREAMSICLES

These creamy, dreamy strawberry pops have a hint of basil for a nice surprise. You can also turn this recipe into a lovely milkshake! Just use cold ingredients and add some ice when you blend.

 NF MAKES 6

2 cups (480 ml) fresh strawberries
1 (14-ounce/400 ml) can full-fat coconut milk
2 tablespoons maple syrup or other sweetener
10 to 15 fresh basil leaves

Place all the ingredients in a blender and blend until smooth. Taste and add more basil or sweetener, if desired. Pour into ice pop molds, add ice pop sticks, and freeze for 4 to 6 hours, until firm. Remove the molds by dipping them into hot water for a moment. Serve and enjoy!

BLUEBERRY CREAMSICLES

Blueberries are always a good idea, especially with ice cream!

 NF MAKES 8

1 cup (240 ml) full-fat coconut milk
½ cup (120 ml) oat milk or other plant-based milk
3 tablespoons rice syrup or other sweetener
1 teaspoon vanilla extract
½ cup (120 ml) fresh blueberries

Blend the coconut milk, oat milk, rice syrup, and vanilla in a blender or whisk in a bowl. Drop blueberries into ice pop molds and fill the molds with the coconut mixture. Add ice pop sticks and place the molds in the freezer for about 4 hours, or until they are solid. Remove the molds by dipping them into hot water for a moment. Serve and enjoy!

KIWI-LIME SORBET

Here's a super-fresh sorbet for all you kiwi lovers! Kiwi is naturally tart, so to keep this from being too tangy, make sure to use kiwis that are very ripe and soft, and taste the mixture before freezing to make sure you've added enough sweetness. If you want it sweeter naturally, toss a banana in there!

 NF · SERVES 2

6 ripe kiwifruit, peeled and chopped
1 ripe avocado, peeled and diced
Juice of 1 lime
5 fresh mint leaves
5 tablespoons coconut syrup or other sweetener

Combine all the ingredients in a blender and puree until smooth. Taste and add more sweetener, if desired.

With an ice cream maker:
Pour the mixture into an ice cream maker and prepare according to the manufacturer's instructions. Serve immediately or transfer to a freezer-safe container, cover, and freeze until ready to serve. Let the sorbet thaw for 10 to 15 minutes before serving.

Without an ice cream maker:
Pour the mixture into a freezer-safe bowl and freeze for about 3 hours, mixing well every 30 minutes. Scoop into bowls, serve, and enjoy!

Quick tip! If you have a high-speed blender, peel and chop the kiwifruit and avocado into small pieces and freeze them first. Then puree the frozen fruits with the rest of the ingredients in a blender until smooth, and serve it immediately as soft sorbet!

MANGO-COCONUT ICE POPS

When you've got ripe mangoes, there's only one solution: Turn them into ice cream!

 NF MAKES 6

**2 ripe mangoes
1 (14-ounce/400-ml) can full-fat coconut milk (refrigerated overnight)
1 to 2 tablespoons maple syrup or other sweetener, if needed**

Peel and chop the mangoes and place them in a blender. Open the coconut milk can and scoop the thick white cream into a blender. Blend until smooth and creamy. Taste and add sweetener, if needed. Pour into ice pop molds, add ice pop sticks, and freeze for 4 to 6 hours, until firm. Remove the molds by dipping them into hot water for a moment. Serve and enjoy!

CHERRY-AMARETTO CREAMSICLES

If you love sweet treats with a hint of booze (and who doesn't?), try these. Feel free to sub almond extract for the almond liqueur—the flavor pairs very well with cherries.

 NF MAKES 8

2 cups (480 ml) fresh red cherries, pitted
1 tablespoon fresh lemon juice
5 tablespoons maple syrup or other sweetener
1 teaspoon amaretto liqueur or almond extract
2 (14-ounce/400-ml) cans full-fat coconut milk (refrigerated overnight)
2 tablespoons coconut butter
1 teaspoon vanilla extract

Combine the cherries, lemon juice, maple syrup, and almond liqueur in a blender and blend until smooth. Pour about half the cherry mixture into the bottoms of ice pop molds and freeze for about 1 hour.

While the cherry mixture is chilling, open the coconut milk cans, scoop out the thick white cream, and whisk it in a bowl with the coconut butter and vanilla extract until creamy. Spoon in the remainder of the cherry mixture and mix gently, so that you get a marbled effect. Evenly divide the mixture among the ice pop molds. Insert ice pop sticks, return ice pops to the freezer, and freeze for about 3 hours, or until solid. Serve and enjoy!

ZESTY ORANGE CREAMSICLES

*A simple, quick, and fun snack on a hot
day or after a sweaty workout!*

 NF MAKES 5

1 orange
1 peach, pit removed
1 cup (240 ml) unsweetened
almond milk
1 tablespoon rice syrup
1 teaspoon vanilla extract
1 teaspoon grated fresh ginger

Peel the orange and remove the pith
(white, bitter membrane) and seeds.
Combine all the ingredients in a
blender and blend until smooth.
Pour the mixture into ice pop molds
and freeze for about 3 hours, or
until solid. Remove the molds by
dipping them into hot water for a
moment. Serve and enjoy!

BREAKFAST ICE POPS

*We think ice cream is a reasonable breakfast,
especially in the form of these yummy breakfast Popsicles!*

MAKES 6

1 cup (240 ml) mixed fresh fruit
and berries
1 teaspoon vanilla extract
2 cups (480 ml) coconut yogurt
or other plant-based yogurt
½ to 1 cup (120 to 240 ml)
Homemade Granola (page 193)

Chop the fruit into small pieces.
Stir the vanilla extract into the
yogurt with a spoon. Alternate
layers of the fruit and coconut
yogurt in ice pop molds, leaving
some space for granola. Add the
granola, press down lightly, and add
ice pop sticks. Place the molds in
the freezer for 4 to 6 hours or until
frozen. Remove the molds by dipping
them into hot water for a moment.
Serve and enjoy!

POMEGRANATE-WATERMELON ICE POPS

These ice pops have great personality and a great texture, thanks to the pomegranate seeds.

 NF MAKES 6

1 pomegranate
1 tablespoon maple syrup, if desired
½ watermelon, rind and seeds removed, flesh cut into chunks

Cut the pomegranate in half and remove the seeds. Set aside half the seeds. Put half the seeds in a high-speed blender and add the maple syrup, if desired. Blend until smooth. Divide the pomegranate mixture among 6 ice pop molds and freeze for about 1 hour.

While the ice pops are chilling, puree the watermelon in a blender until smooth. Divide the watermelon mixture among the ice pop molds, and drop the remaining pomegranate seeds on top. Add ice pop sticks, return the ice pops to the freezer, and freeze for 4 to 6 hours, or until solid. Remove the molds by dipping them into hot water for a moment. Serve and enjoy!

4

MILKSHAKES

Forget smoothies. Milkshakes are back, baby! Only now we're using plant-based milks and other nice goodies, so they're healthy, too!

$5 Milkshake

Super-Simple Strawberry Milkshake

Chai Milkshake

Minty Triple-Chocolate Milkshake

Piña Colada Milkshake

Salted Caramel Milkshake

$5 MILKSHAKE

A legendary milkshake from the movie Pulp Fiction *is now a bit healthier but still just as badass.*

"I don't know if that shake's worth five dollars,
but it's pretty damn good."
—Vincent Vega, *Pulp Fiction*

SERVES 1

1 (14-ounce / 400ml) full-fat coconut milk (refrigerated overnight)
½ cup (120 ml) unsweetened almond milk
2 frozen bananas
Seeds from 1 bourbon vanilla bean, or ½ teaspoon vanilla powder
1 tablespoon coconut syrup
4 ice cubes
Coconut Whipped Cream (page 185)
Cherry, for garnish

Open the coconut milk can and scoop ½ cup (120 ml) of the thick white cream into a blender. Add the almond milk, bananas, vanilla, coconut syrup, and ice cubes and blend until smooth. Pour into a tall glass. Drop some Coconut Whipped Cream on top and finish with a cherry. Serve and enjoy!

Hint! Make the milkshake extra delicious by adding one scoop of Vanilla Ice Cream.

Vanilla Ice Cream

2 (14-ounce/400-ml) cans full-fat coconut milk (refrigerated overnight)
2 tablespoons coconut palm syrup or other sweetener
1 teaspoon vanilla extract

Open the coconut milk cans and scoop the thick white cream into a blender. Add the coconut palm syrup and vanilla extract. Blend until smooth. Pour the mixture into an ice cream maker and prepare according to the manufacturer's instructions, or pour the mixture into a freezer-safe bowl and freeze for about 3 hours, mixing every 30 minutes until the ice cream is ready. Serve and enjoy!

SUPER-SIMPLE STRAWBERRY MILKSHAKE

This amazingly easy and tasty milkshake requires only three ingredients! For extra sweetness, blend in a ripe banana.

SERVES 2

1 (14-ounce/400-ml) can full-fat coconut milk
1 cup (240 ml) frozen strawberries
1 teaspoon vanilla extract

Combine all the ingredients in a blender and blend until smooth. Serve and enjoy!

Tip! Spoon in some Coconut Whipped Cream (page 185) for extra creaminess and pretty swirls!

CHAI MILKSHAKE

*A soothing and calming chai latte,
in the form of a milkshake.*

 NF SERVES 1

1 bag herbal chai tea
1½ frozen bananas
1 cup (240 ml) unsweetened almond
milk or other plant-based milk
1 to 2 fresh dates, pitted
1 teaspoon ground Ceylon cinnamon

Cut the tea bag open and pour the
contents into a blender. Add the
remaining ingredients and blend
until smooth. Taste and add more
spices or sweetener, if desired.
Serve and enjoy!

MINTY TRIPLE-CHOCOLATE MILKSHAKE

 SERVES 2

Chocolate foam:
1 recipe Coconut Whipped Cream (page 185), whipped with
3 tablespoons raw cacao powder or unsweetened cocoa powder

Milkshake:
3 frozen bananas
1½ cups (360 ml) almond milk or other plant-based milk
3 tablespoons raw cacao powder or unsweetened cocoa powder
6 fresh mint leaves
1 teaspoon vanilla extract

Chocolate sauce:
3 tablespoons extra virgin coconut oil
3 tablespoons raw cacao powder
1 tablespoon coconut syrup or other sweetener
½ teaspoon peppermint oil
Pinch of sea salt

Prepare the chocolate foam first, and set aside.

To make the milkshake, combine all the milkshake ingredients in a blender and blend until smooth.

To make the chocolate sauce, melt the coconut oil until soft. Add the remaining ingredients and whisk until smooth.

Pour some of the chocolate sauce into two glasses. Fill each glass halfway with the milkshake mixture. Spoon in some of the chocolate foam. Fill the glass the rest of the way with milkshake. Top with chocolate foam and chocolate sauce. Serve and enjoy!

N'Ice Cream

PIÑA COLADA
MILKSHAKE

Take a sip of this tropical milkshake
and swoosh into the sun!

 SERVES 2

1 (14-ounce/400-ml) can full-fat
coconut milk (refrigerated
overnight)
2 frozen bananas
¾ cup (180 ml) pineapple, fresh or
canned
1 teaspoon vanilla extract
3 ice cubes

Open the coconut milk can and scoop
the thick white cream into a blender.
Add the remaining ingredients and
blend until smooth. Serve and enjoy!

SALTED CARAMEL MILKSHAKE

A creamy cashew milkshake with sweet 'n' salty caramel sauce is definitely on the top of our daydreams!

SERVES 2

½ cup (120 ml) cashew nuts (soaked overnight or for at least 4 hours, optional)
2 frozen bananas
1½ cups (360 ml) unsweetened almond milk or other plant-based milk
1 teaspoon vanilla extract
½ cup (120 ml) Caramel Sauce (page 182)
Coconut Whipped Cream (page 185), for serving, optional

We prefer the cashews soaked, but if you're pressed for time you can skip the soaking. Rinse and drain the cashews and place them in a blender with the bananas, almond milk, and vanilla and blend until smooth. Pour some Caramel Sauce into two glasses, then divide the milkshake between the glasses and decorate with the remaining Caramel Sauce. Top with Coconut Whipped Cream, if desired. Serve and enjoy!

○ ○ ○ ○ ⑤ ○

ICE CREAM CAKES AND COOKIES

Celebrate life with these ultimate treats.

Dreamy Blackberry Ice Cream Cake

Cherry Ice Cream Cake

Raw Chocolate Ice Cream Cookies

Chocolate-Blueberry Ice Cream Cups

Caramel-Peanut Ice Cream Cake

Mint Chocolate Ice Cream Sandwiches

Berry Cookie Crumble Ice Cream Cups

Vanilla-Raspberry Ice Cream Cookies

DREAMY BLACKBERRY ICE CREAM CAKE

This cake is to die for. It's a cinch to throw together, and looks so beautiful when you break it out at a party. If you aren't as concerned with presentation and just want to eat it as soon as possible, you can also make the filling as a normal ice cream—just sprinkle the crust on top of the ice cream and spoon the magic into your mouth!

SERVES 6

Cake Crumble (page 186)

1 cup (240 ml) fresh blackberries
1 (14-ounce/400-ml) can full-fat coconut milk (refrigerated overnight)
½ cup (120 ml) cashew nuts
2 tablespoons maple syrup or other sweetener
½ teaspoon vanilla powder
1 tablespoon fresh lemon juice

Line a 6-inch (17-cm) springform cake pan with parchment paper. Press the cake crumble into the bottom of the pan. Set aside.

Mash the blackberries with a fork, leaving aside a few whole ones for decoration. Set aside.

Open the coconut milk can and scoop the thick white cream into a blender. Add the cashews, maple syrup, vanilla, and lemon juice and blend until smooth. Pour the mixture into a bowl and swirl in the blackberry mash. Pour the mixture into the prepared cake pan. Place the pan in the freezer and freeze for about 3 hours, or until the cake is solid. Remove the cake from the pan and let thaw for 10 to 15 minutes, then decorate with the reserved blackberries. Serve and enjoy!

CHERRY ICE CREAM CAKE

This is a tribute to Linda Lomelino, one of the greatest food bloggers and photographers of our time. The cake is a variant of one from her ice cream book Lomelinos Glass. *This creamy cherry cake most certainly makes a party!*

 NF SERVES 6

Ice cream:
1½ cups (360 ml) fresh cherries, pitted
1 cup (240 ml) hemp seeds or cashew nuts
1 ripe banana
⅓ cup (80 ml) unsweetened almond milk or other plant-based milk
5 tablespoons coconut palm syrup or other sweetener
1 teaspoon vanilla extract
¼ cup extra virgin coconut oil, melted

Chocolate frosting:
1 cup (240 ml) grated cacao butter
5 tablespoons extra virgin coconut oil
5 tablespoons raw cacao powder or unsweetened cocoa powder
2 tablespoons coconut palm syrup or other sweetener
Pinch of sea salt

1 Gluten-Free Waffle Ice Cream Cone (page 197), for serving

Line a 6-inch (17-cm) springform cake pan with parchment paper. Set aside.

Combine all the ice cream ingredients in a blender or food processor and blend until smooth. Pour the mixture into an ice cream maker and prepare according to the manufacturer's instructions. You can also pour the mixture into a bowl and freeze for about 3 hours, mixing every 30 minutes. Remove one big scoop of ice cream and reserve it in the freezer. to use as decoration later Press the rest of the ice cream into the prepared cake pan and put into the freezer for 1 to 2 hours or until solid. In the meantime, prepare the chocolate frosting.

Melt the cacao butter and coconut oil in a small saucepan over medium-low heat. Remove from the heat and add the cacao powder, coconut palm syrup, and salt and stir. Taste and add sweetener, if desired.

Remove the cake from the freezer and remove from the cake pan. Place the reserved ice cream scoop in a waffle cone and press it into the middle of the cake. Pour the chocolate frosting on the cake with a spoon so that it covers the ice cream ball and the surface of the cake. Let the chocolate frosting dribble a little bit down the sides, too. Serve and enjoy!

RAW CHOCOLATE ICE CREAM COOKIES

Sometimes, all you need is chocolate. And other times, chocolate on chocolate is required. Make sure you cut these cookies into small servings or else they'll be gone in seconds!

MAKES  COOKIES

Raw chocolate cookies:
2 cups (480 ml) walnuts
2 tablespoons raw cacao powder or unsweetened cocoa powder
Pinch of sea salt
12 to 14 fresh dates, pitted
Splash of coconut syrup, optional

Creamy chocolate ice cream:
1 (14-ounce/400-ml) can full-fat coconut milk (refrigerated overnight)
2 frozen bananas
2 to 4 tablespoons raw cacao powder or unsweetened cocoa powder
2 tablespoons maple syrup or other sweetener

Line a 6 x 8-inch (14 x 20-cm) loaf pan with plastic wrap and set aside.

Combine the walnuts, cacao powder, and sea salt in a blender or a food processor and pulse to form fine crumbs. Add the dates and pulse until a sticky dough forms. Add coconut syrup, if desired. Divide the cookie dough in half. Press half the dough firmly into the bottom of the prepared loaf pan and place in the freezer. Meanwhile, make the ice cream.

Open the coconut milk can and scoop the thick white cream into a blender. Add the bananas, cacao powder, and maple syrup and blend until smooth, scraping down the sides of the blender if necessary. Taste and add more maple syrup or cacao, if desired.

When the ice cream is ready, take the loaf pan from the freezer and spread the ice cream evenly on top of the cookie layer. Return to the freezer and freeze for 2 to 4 hours, or until solid. Press the remaining cookie dough evenly on top of the ice cream. Freeze for another 2 to 4 hours, or until frozen.

When ready to serve, take the pan from the freezer and, with the help of the plastic wrap, remove the cookie sandwich from the loaf pan. Cut into pieces with a sharp knife, serve, and enjoy!

CHOCOLATE-BLUEBERRY ICE CREAM CUPS

This concoction of raw chocolate combined with creamy coconut will literally melt in your mouth.

 NF MAKES 6

1 (14-ounce/400-ml) can full-fat coconut milk (refrigerated overnight)
2 tablespoons extra virgin coconut oil
1 tablespoon maple syrup or other sweetener
¼ teaspoon vanilla extract
½ cup fresh blueberries

Raw chocolate topping:
2 tablespoons raw cacao butter
2 tablespoons extra virgin coconut oil
2 tablespoons coconut palm syrup or other sweetener
3 to 4 tablespoons raw cacao powder

½ teaspoon vanilla extract
Pinch of sea salt

Open the coconut milk can and scoop the thick white cream into a blender. Add the coconut oil, maple syrup, and vanilla and blend until smooth. Taste and add more syrup or vanilla, if desired. Pour into silicone muffin cups and scatter the blueberries evenly across the top, leaving some room for the chocolate topping. Put the cups in the freezer while you make the chocolate topping.

Melt the cacao butter and coconut oil in a small saucepan over medium-low heat. Remove from the heat and whisk in the coconut syrup, raw cacao powder, vanilla, and sea salt.

Remove the muffin cups from the freezer, cover with the chocolate topping, and return to the freezer. Freeze for 2 to 4 hours, or until solid. Remove the silicone cups, serve, and enjoy!

CARAMEL-PEANUT ICE CREAM CAKE

This ice cream cake was created after a request from one of our readers who wanted a healthier version of her favorite ice cream flavor, Snickers. The outcome was magnificent; we hope all you peanut and chocolate lovers will fall in love with this as deeply as we did!

SERVES 6

Ice cream:
1 (14-ounce/400-ml) can full-fat coconut milk (refrigerated overnight)
3 ripe bananas
½ cup (120 ml) peanut butter
1 teaspoon vanilla extract
Handful of raw peanuts
Pinch of sea salt

Caramel filling:
½ cup (120 ml) peanut butter
10 fresh dates, pitted
4 tablespoons extra virgin coconut oil
⅔ cup (160 ml) full-fat coconut milk
½ teaspoon vanilla extract
Pinch sea salt

Chocolate sauce frosting (page 182)
Crushed hazelnuts, for garnish

Line a 3.5 x 7.5-inch (9 x 19-cm) loaf pan with parchment paper. Set aside.

Open the coconut milk can and scoop the thick white cream into a blender. Add the bananas, peanut butter, and vanilla and blend until smooth. Pour the ice cream mixture into the prepared loaf pan. In a small bowl, mix the peanuts with the salt, scatter the mixture on top of the ice cream, and set aside.

Combine all the caramel filling ingredients in a blender and blend until smooth, adding more water if needed to achieve the consistency of a smooth caramel sauce. Pour about half the caramel filling over the ice cream. Reserve the remaining caramel filling. Place the pan into a freezer for about 3 hours, or until solid.

Remove the ice cream cake from the pan and place it onto a serving plate. Pour the reserved caramel filling on top, then pour the chocolate frosting over the caramel sauce. Sprinkle with some crushed hazelnuts. Let the cake thaw slightly (this will make it easier to cut), serve, and enjoy!

MINT CHOCOLATE ICE CREAM SANDWICHES

Mint and chocolate are one of our favorite combinations in treats, and these ice cream sandwiches are a fantastic way to have a minty delight.

(NF) MAKES **6-8** ICE CREAM SANDWICHES

Chocolate cookies:
¾ cup (180 ml) almond flour
½ cup (120 ml) gluten-free oat flour
½ cup (120 ml) buckwheat flour
3 tablespoons raw cacao powder or unsweetened cocoa powder
2 tablespoons flaxseed meal
½ teaspoon baking soda
½ teaspoon vanilla extract
Pinch of sea salt
3 tablespoons extra virgin coconut oil
3 to 4 tablespoons maple syrup or other sweetener
¼ cup water

Mint ice cream:
2 (14-ounce/400-ml) cans full-fat coconut milk (refrigerated overnight)

2 ripe avocados, peeled and diced
5 to 7 tablespoons maple syrup or other sweetener
1 teaspoon peppermint extract
Big handful of fresh mint leaves

Preheat the oven to 350°F (175°C). Mix all the dry ingredients in a big bowl. In a small saucepan, melt the coconut oil over medium-low heat until runny. Add the coconut oil, maple syrup, vanilla, and water to the dry ingredients and mix well until a sticky dough forms, adding more flour if necessary. Let the dough thicken for a few minutes. You should

be able to make a big ball out of the dough with your hands.

Divide the dough in half and place one half between two pieces of parchment paper. Roll out to ½-inch thickness. Cut the dough into rectangles and place on a baking sheet. Repeat with the remaining dough.

Bake for 8 to 12 minutes. Allow to cool completely. The cookies can be a bit soft when you take them from the oven but they will get crispier as they cool.

Hint! For a nut-free version, replace the almond flour with more oat and buckwheat flour!

Open the coconut milk
cans and scoop the
thick white cream into
a blender. Add the
remaining ingredients
and blend until smooth.
Pour the mixture into an
ice cream maker and
prepare according to
the manufacturer's
instructions, or pour the
mixture into a freezer-safe
bowl and freeze for about
3 hours, mixing well every
30 minutes.

Assembling the cookies:
Scoop a spoonful of the
ice cream and place it on
the back side of one
cookie. Place another
cookie on top of the ice
cream and press down
gently. Repeat with the
remaining cookies to
form 6 to 8 ice cream
sandwiches. Enjoy right
away or freeze for 1 hour,
if you like them firmer.

BERRY COOKIE CRUMBLE ICE CREAM CUPS

These little ice cream cups are perfect for parties.
They're really easy to make as well!

MAKES **8**

Ice cream:
1 cup (240 ml) cashew nuts or almonds (soaked overnight or for at least 4 to 6 hours)
1 cup (240 ml) fresh raspberries or strawberries
1 cup (240 ml) unsweetened almond milk or other plant-based milk
2 tablespoons fresh lemon juice
2 to 3 tablespoons maple syrup or other sweetener
½ teaspoon vanilla extract
Cake Crumble (page 186)

Rinse and drain the cashews. Combine them with all the other ingredients in a blender and blend until smooth and creamy. Taste and add more sweetener if desired. Divide the mixture evenly among eight ice pop molds or silicone muffin cups, leaving room for the cake crumble. Freeze for 1 hour, or until quite solid.

While the ice pops are freezing, prepare the cake crumble.

Remove the ice cream pops or cups from the freezer and sprinkle with the cake crumble. Insert ice pop sticks into the middle of each pop or cup and freeze for 2 hours, until solid. Run the molds or cups quickly through hot water to loosen, serve, and enjoy!

VANILLA-RASPBERRY ICE CREAM COOKIES

Gluten-free oat cookies with creamy vanilla ice cream will melt anyone's heart. But be quick, before the ice cream melts!

MAKES **12** COOKIES
6 ICE CREAM COOKIES

Gluten-free oat thins:
¾ cup (180 ml) gluten-free rolled oats
½ cup (120 ml) gluten-free oat flour
¼ cup extra virgin coconut oil, melted
2 tablespoons maple syrup or other sweetener
¼ cup oat milk or other plant-based milk
Pinch sea salt

Ice cream:
1 recipe Creamy Vanilla Ice Cream (page 49)
¾ cup (180 ml) fresh raspberries

Preheat the oven to 400°F (200°C). Line a baking sheet with parchment paper and set aside.

Mix all the cookie ingredients in a big bowl. The dough should be quite sticky. Drop the dough onto the prepared baking sheet, creating 12 cookies total. Flatten them out as thin as possible. Bake for 10 to 15 minutes, or until golden. Remove the cookies from the baking sheet and cool completely before filling.

Make the vanilla ice cream according to the instructions on page 49 and add fresh raspberries just before the ice cream is ready or before freezing in a container. Let thaw for a moment so it's easier to scoop.

To make the ice cream cookies, place a cookie on a plate, scoop some ice cream on top, set another cookie on top, and press together slightly. Serve and enjoy!

Hint! Try these cookies with other creamy ice cream flavors, too.

ADDITIONS AND TOPPINGS

If you want to make your ice cream extra luxurious, add some of these toppings!

Chocolate Sauce

White Chocolate Sauce

Caramel Sauce

Coconut Whipped Cream

Cake Crumble

Chocolate Cake Crumble

Berry Jam

Berry Sauce

Oat Ice Cream Bowls

Homemade Granola

Chocolate Cookie Cups

Gluten-Free Waffle Ice Cream Cones and Cups

CHOCOLATE SAUCE

This raw chocolate sauce is super simple and quick to make. You can use it as a topping for your ice cream, or dip frozen ice pops in the sauce to get a nice chocolate glaze.

½ cup (120 ml) raw cacao butter, melted
¼ cup (60 ml) extra virgin coconut oil, melted
5 tablespoons raw cacao powder
3 to 4 tablespoons coconut syrup or other sweetener
Pinch of sea salt

Place all the ingredients in a small bowl and whisk into a smooth sauce. Taste and add more sweetener, if desired.

WHITE CHOCOLATE SAUCE

This sauce is for white-chocolate lovers. It makes a pretty glaze!

1 cup (240 ml) raw cacao butter, melted
1 cup (240 ml) raw macadamia nuts
¼ cup (60 ml) coconut syrup
Splash of coconut milk, unsweetened almond milk, or water, optional

Combine the cacao butter, macadamia nuts, and coconut syrup in a high-speed blender and process until smooth. Add a little bit of coconut milk if the mixture is too thick.

CARAMEL SAUCE

This natural caramel sauce with a date base is super delicious and perfect mixed into or on top of ice cream!

8 fresh dates, pitted
2 tablespoons extra virgin coconut oil
¼ cup (60 ml) water
½ teaspoon vanilla extract
Pinch sea salt

Combine all the ingredients in a blender and blend until smooth. Add more water, if needed, to achieve the consistency of a smooth caramel sauce, or add even more water if you desire a runnier sauce.

Hint! To make the sauce extra creamy, add 2 tablespoons coconut milk!

COCONUT WHIPPED CREAM

Whipped cream is a great partner to ice cream. This dairy-free version is even better than the original!

 NF MAKES ABOUT 2 CUPS

2 (14-ounce/400-ml) cans full-fat coconut milk (refrigerated overnight)
½ teaspoon vanilla powder
Few drops stevia (or other sweetener)

Open the coconut milk cans and scoop the thick white cream into a bowl and beat until fluffy. Mix in the vanilla and stevia. Use immediately. (If the mixture is too runny, place it in the refrigerator for about 15 minutes.)

Store leftovers, covered, in the refrigerator; use within 3 days.

CAKE CRUMBLE

Sprinkle this raw cake crumble on your ice creams as a topping, roll your ice cream balls in it for a crunchy outer layer, or add it to your ice cream batter to vary the texture.

1 cup (240 ml) macadamia nuts or your favorite mixed nuts—cashews, pecans, almonds, etc.
2 to 3 fresh dates, pitted
½ teaspoon ground cardamom
Pinch of sea salt
1 tablespoon coconut syrup, optional

Combine all the ingredients in a blender and pulse until fine crumbs form. Taste and add more sweetener if desired.

Nut-free version:
Instead of nuts, use ½ cup (120 ml) rolled oats and ½ cup (120 ml) dried mulberries.

Chocolate Cake Crumble

½ cup (120 ml) rolled oats
½ cup (120 ml) almonds
2 fresh dates, pitted
¼ cup (60 ml) raw cacao powder
Pinch of sea salt
1 tablespoon coconut syrup

Combine all the ingredients in a blender and pulse until fine crumbs form. Taste and add more sweetener, if desired.

Nut-free version:
Instead of almonds, use ½ cup (120 ml) dried mulberries.

The same delicious cake crumbs, but with chocolate flavor!

BERRY JAM

If you'd like to add a bit of sweetness to your ice cream, try this simple berry jam.

1 cup (240 ml) mixed berries
2 to 3 tablespoons maple syrup or other sweetener
½ cup (120 ml) water
3 tablespoons chia seeds
Vanilla extract, optional
Lemon juice and/or lemon peel, optional
Fresh berries, for serving, optional

Combine the berries, maple syrup, and water in a blender and blend for 20 to 30 seconds, making sure that there are still some berry seeds left. Pour into a bowl, add the chia seeds, and stir well. Add the vanilla and/or lemon peel, if using, and stir gently. Place in the refrigerator for about 1 hour, or until the jam has thickened. Add some fresh berries before serving, if desired.

BERRY SAUCE

This fresh berry sauce is a perfect accompaniment to all ice cream flavors.

2 cups (240 ml) strawberries or other berries
Juice of 1 lemon
2 tablespoons maple syrup or other sweetener

Combine all the ingredients in a blender and blend until smooth.

OAT ICE CREAM BOWLS

These simple edible serving bowls are easy to put together, and make your sundae that much more impressive and delicious. If you're on a raw diet, you can make these with a food dehydrator and keep them raw. Otherwise, they're very easy to bake!

NF MAKES 6-8

Coconut oil, for greasing the muffin tin
1 large ripe banana
2 cups (480 ml) gluten-free rolled oats or raw oat groats
5 fresh dates, pitted
1 teaspoon vanilla powder
Pinch of sea salt

Preheat the oven to 230°F (110°C). Turn a muffin tin upside down and grease the outside of the shells with coconut oil and set aside.

Place the banana, oats, dates, vanilla, and salt in a food processor and process until a ball starts to form (you can also use a high-speed blender and prepare the dough in two batches).

Divide the dough into 6 to 8 small balls and press them against the outer shells of the tins so that they form a bowl shape. Bake for about 15 to 25 minutes, depending on how thick you made the bowls. When ready, the bowls should feel dry. Then let them cool until it's possible to gently remove the cups from the tin, helping with a knife if needed, and invert them to cool completely. Fill with ice cream and enjoy!

If you follow a raw food diet: Instead of baking, place the bowls in a food dehydrator set to 115°F (45°C) for about 8 hours. Remove the bowls from the shells of the muffin tin and dehydrate for 8 hours more. The bowls are ready when they are not sticky to the touch. Store in an airtight container and use within 1 week.

HOMEMADE GRANOLA

Try this simple granola as an ice cream topping or to add some crunch to your ice pops!

MAKES **12** SERVINGS

2 cups (480 ml) gluten-free rolled oats
½ cup (120 ml) almonds
½ cup (120 ml) pecans or other nuts
½ cup (120 ml) hemp seeds or other seeds
½ cup (120 ml) extra virgin coconut oil, melted
¼ cup (60 ml) maple syrup or other sweetener
1 teaspoon vanilla extract
½ teaspoon sea salt

Preheat the oven to 375°F (190°C). Line a baking sheet with parchment paper and set aside.

In a large bowl, combine the oats, almonds, pecans, and seeds. In a separate bowl, combine the coconut oil, maple syrup, vanilla, and salt. Combine both mixtures and pour onto the prepared baking sheet.

Bake for 20 to 25 minutes, stirring once, to achieve an even color.

Let cool completely. Store in an airtight container at room temperature for up to 1 month.

CHOCOLATE COOKIE CUPS

When you're looking for a fun and delicious way to serve your ice cream, make these chocolate cookie cups!

MAKES 6-8

Coconut oil, for greasing
1 big ripe banana
1 cup (240 ml) gluten-free rolled oats
½ cup (120 ml) almond flour
3 tablespoons raw cacao powder or unsweetened cocoa powder
5 fresh dates, pitted
1 teaspoon vanilla extract
Pinch of sea salt

Preheat the oven to 225°F (110°C). Turn a muffin tin upside down and grease the outside of the wells with coconut oil. Set aside.

Combine all the ingredients in a blender or food processor and pulse until a sticky dough forms. (If using a blender, you can prepare the dough in two batches.)

Divide the dough into 6 to 8 small balls and press them against the outer shells of the tins so that they form a bowl shape. Bake them for about 20 to 30 minutes, then let them cool until it's possible to gently remove them from the tin and invert the cups to cool completely. Fill with ice cream and enjoy!

GLUTEN-FREE WAFFLE ICE CREAM CONES AND CUPS

Homemade waffle ice cream cones take your ice cream experience to a whole new level. You can also make waffle cups by pressing the waffle inside of a small bowl before it has hardened.

MAKES 4

3 tablespoons chia seeds
½ cup (120 ml) water
1 cup (240 ml) coconut palm sugar, granulated sugar, or powdered erythritol
1 cup (240 ml) almond flour
6 tablespoons tapioca starch or potato starch
1½ teaspoons vanilla powder
3 tablespoons coconut oil, melted, plus more for greasing the waffle iron

Mix the chia seeds and water in a bowl and let sit for 5 minutes. Add the coconut palm sugar, almond flour, tapioca starch, and vanilla powder. Whisk vigorously so that no lumps remain. Let the mixture thicken for about 5 minutes.

While the mixture sits, prepare cone molds from foil or cardboard paper by cutting about 8-inch (20-cm) squares. Roll the squares into the shape of a cone and tape the edges together. Preheat a waffle iron and grease the surfaces with coconut oil.

When the batter has thickened and the texture resembles porridge, add the melted coconut oil and mix. Spoon 3 to 4 tablespoons batter into the center of the waffle maker and close the lid. Cook the waffles for about 2½ minutes or until golden brown. Lay the waffle onto a cone mold (or cone roller or into a small bowl) and roll the waffle into a cone shape. Let the cone cool for about 2 minutes so that the waffle hardens a bit. Remove gently from the mold and let cool completely on a plate or wire rack. Repeat with the remaining batter.

Tip! Prepare waffle cookies by spooning about 1 tablespoon batter into the center of a waffle maker, cook for 2 to 2½ minutes, then transfer to a plate and let it cool flat.

Forget art.
Put your trust
in ice cream.
—CHARLES BAXTER

THANK YOU!

Foremost, we want to thank you for getting our book!
We hope you've enjoyed reading this book
as much as we loved making it.

We also want to thank our friends and family for helping
us to develop these ice creams by testing and giving
your opinions and ideas. We want to thank Lindsay
Edgecombe, our super-talented agent, and Gabrielle
Campo for trusting our vision and giving us the
opportunity to grow our small project into a real book!
A huge thank-you goes also to all our readers
around the world. We feel so grateful to share
our passion with you and to feel your support,
which keeps us inspired every day!

nicecreambook.com

Also make sure to visit our websites, tuulia.co and vanelja.com,
to keep up with our latest recipes, news, and projects!

INDEX

ABOUT THE AUTHORS

Hi! We are two healthy-food lovers and ice cream enthusiasts. This book was made for the love of frozen treats, as we wanted to share our favorite recipes and inspire others to jump right into the world of healthy cold treats.

Virpi

I'm a recipe artist, a writer, a food stylist, and photographer making cookbooks and running my website, *Vanelja*. At the moment I'm living in Helsinki, Finland, with my four-year-old daughter and my man. They are my best test audience, and I pamper them almost every day with ice creams or other healthy treats. My favorite ice cream from this book must be Salty Caramel Popcorn Ice Cream (page 50). It combines soft and crunchy, sweet and salty, and it's totally addictive!

vanelja.com
instagram.com/vanelja

Tuulia

I'm a natural-foods lover and recipe creator, yogi and yoga teacher, entrepreneur, and a full-time foodie.

I enjoy my life in Helsinki, but I also have a deep passion for traveling and seeing and experiencing new places. I hope to inspire people toward a happier and healthier lifestyle through my everyday work—and, of course, with these awesome ice creams! I have many ice cream favorites, but my current crush is the Avocado 'n' Almond Dream (page 33).

tuulia.co
instagram.com/tuuliatalvio

Your ice cream designers, at your service!